Ohio's Education Reform Challenges

Ohio's Education Reform Challenges

Lessons from the Front Lines

Chester E. Finn, Jr., Terry Ryan,
and Michael B. Lafferty

OHIO'S EDUCATION REFORM CHALLENGES
Copyright © Chester E. Finn, Jr., Terry Ryan, and Michael B. Lafferty, 2010.

All rights reserved.

First published in 2010 by PALGRAVE MACMILLAN® in the United States—a division of St. Martin's Press LLC, 175 Fifth Avenue, New York, NY 10010.

Where this book is distributed in the UK, Europe, and the rest of the world, this is by Palgrave Macmillan, a division of Macmillan Publishers Limited, registered in England, company number 785998, of Houndmills, Basingstoke, Hampshire RG21 6XS.

Palgrave Macmillan is the global academic imprint of the above companies and has companies and representatives throughout the world.

Palgrave® and Macmillan® are registered trademarks in the United States, the United Kingdom, Europe and other countries.

ISBN: 978-0-230-10697-0

Library of Congress Cataloging-in-Publication Data is available from the Library of Congress.

A catalogue record of the book is available from the British Library.

Design by Scribe Inc.

First edition: June 2010

10 9 8 7 6 5 4 3 2 1

Printed in the United States of America.

Contents

Acknowledgments

This book had its genesis the very first day the Thomas B. Fordham Institute opened its doors in Dayton in 1997. The story of Fordham's experiences with charter schools and other education reforms in Ohio would not have been possible without the help of a great number of people who lent perspective and specialized knowledge to the events and history we describe here.

First, we must thank the Fordham trustees, who joined us on this roller coaster and provided guidance and support all along the way. Special thanks to members of the Ohio Policy and Sponsorship Committee, especially Chairman David Driscoll and former chairman Craig Kennedy. Both were invaluable in helping us navigate the choppy education seas of the Buckeye State. Thanks also to board member Tom Holton and his colleague Chas Kidwell at the law firm Porter, Wright, Morris & Arthur for their essential help and guidance with the innumerable legal challenges of a charter school sponsor.

We're grateful, too, to the library staff at the *Columbus Dispatch* for their indefatigable help in getting the background right. Concerning the history of Dayton, Dr. Gary LeRoy was generous with his memories of growing up in the city during integration. University of Dayton professor Joseph Watras provided background on the school desegregation saga. Veteran Dayton educators Richard Penry and Tim Nealon offered firsthand knowledge of their experience as teachers and administrators in that city's school system.

Susan Stibbing and Ron Budzik helped us understand the Dayton business community's myriad efforts to revitalize the city school system. Former Board of Education president Gail Littlejohn and former superintendent James Williams provided us with immeasurable help in understanding Dayton's school reform efforts, as did current superintendent Kurt Stanic. *Dayton Daily News* reporters Scott Elliott and Mark Fisher helped with firsthand journalism on innumerable education developments in the community.

In seeking to understand the state-level political process, we benefited greatly from Lee Leonard, a former *Columbus Dispatch* statehouse reporter, as well as from Ohio senators Jon Husted and Jeff Jacobson, former state auditor Jim Petro, and former governor Bob Taft. *Dispatch* reporters Catherine Candisky and Joe Hallett helped immeasurably with their coverage of the DeRolfe school funding case and other statewide issues.

In reconstructing Fordham's own protracted deliberations on charter school sponsorship, we thank board members Bruno V. Manno and David H. Ponitz for their insights and recollections. Reverend Vanessa Ward, of the Omega Baptist Church, was very helpful with perspectives on the difficulties of founding and running a charter school.

In all, more than two dozen people provided firsthand knowledge in interviews for the book. In addition to those named above, we thank John Gower, planning director, and Diane Shannon, economist, for the City of Dayton; Tyrone Thornton, a teacher at Thurgood Marshall High; and Dayton businessmen and civic leaders Matt Diggs, Allen Hill, and Mike Ervin, all of whose personal experiences helped explain a complex story.

For research assistance, we're especially grateful to Fordham staffers Emmy L. Partin, Director of Ohio Policy and Research; Jamie Davies O'Leary, Ohio policy and research analyst; and Eric Ulas, Ohio policy and research associate.

Special thanks also to our colleagues Kathryn Mullen Upton, director of charter school sponsorship; Theda Sampson, program administrator; and Whitney Gilbert, staff assistant; as well as to Fordham, DC, staffers Mike Petrilli, Eric Osberg, Marci Kanstoroom, and Laura Pohl for their help, support, and encouragement along the way.

Finally, Thomas J. Lasley, dean of the School of Education and Allied Professions at the University of Dayton, provided welcome help in reviewing the manuscript, and, for that, we are very grateful. Thanks to Rick Hess of the American Enterprise Institute for his help in finding a suitable publisher for this book and to Burke Gerstenschlager at Palgrave Macmillan for shepherding it through the publication process.

Introduction

In the Thomas B. Fordham Institute's customary role as a bumptious education-reform think tank and advocacy organization, operating primarily at the national level, we don't have enough contact with the real world of transforming schools, educating children, and negotiating with legislators. Getting down and dirty in Ohio's education-reform struggles over the past dozen years has proved eye-opening and sobering.

Theorists don't necessarily fare well in the world of politics, organizational interests, trial and error, and human frailty. Experts' theories don't always hold water. Their ivory tower experience doesn't necessarily translate. Yet Fordham's engagement in Ohio—beginning in its hometown of Dayton—has proved deeply instructive. We've learned a ton from our many efforts, not all of them successful, to reform urban education, to help launch new schools, to fix broken older schools, to assist needy families to make their way into better education options—and to duke it out with powerful institutional resistances and adult interests that don't want the status quo to change in the ways we think would benefit children.

This book represents our very best effort to describe and analyze those efforts and distill from our Ohio experience a manageable set of lessons that can benefit others who share our goal of transforming education in the Buckeye State and across America.

It's also the result of a commitment we made to the Bill and Melinda Gates Foundation in May 2005 when we sought their help in our then-new role as a charter school authorizer. We had big dreams for what we might accomplish in that capacity but knew we couldn't make a go of it—at least not in the ways it needed to be done—without outside support. In return for that support (which Gates generously provided), we promised to chronicle all that we learned that might enhance the national charter enterprise.

Ohio is one of just two states where nonprofit organizations like Fordham may sponsor charter schools. Sponsorship—also known as authorizing—is the least understood element of the charter world. How organizations such as ours might function in that capacity is unmapped terrain. Plenty of education reformers, policymakers, philanthropists, and scholars—ourselves included—want to know more about it: what works and what doesn't; what's possible, impossible, and unanticipated. What happens when an organization tries to shift from talking the talk of school reform to walking the walk in a real place like southwestern Ohio?

Fordham is pretty good at talking the talk and easily could have stuck to that "core competency." We keep plenty busy with national studies as well as policy analyses in Ohio. We didn't have to take on sponsorship. Indeed, doubts were voiced that we could do this well. Doubts even within our own board came to the surface. Former trustee Diane Ravitch, the respected education historian (and Chester Finn's longtime friend and collaborator), summed up this skepticism in 2006 when she told a journalist "I don't think think tanks should run schools, but I was outvoted."

After much deliberation and some palpitations (e.g., liability and reputation concerns, staff capacity, budget constraints), Fordham took on the sponsor's role for five compelling reasons:

- We knew Ohio had a shortage of quality sponsors, which portended trouble for the state's charter school effort.
- We wanted to encourage high-quality charter operators to come to Ohio at a time when too many district-run schools (and homegrown charters) were faltering, particularly when it came to educating poor and minority youngsters.
- We believed—and continue to believe—that charters can play a critical role in nudging school districts to innovate and improve.
- We suspected we could learn a lot from the experience and might be able to share these lessons.
- Most important, we believed that quality charter schools throw a crucial lifeline to children otherwise stuck in failing schools. This has long been evident in Dayton, but the more time we spent in Ohio's other major urban centers, the clearer it became that this is a statewide condition.

Our story is more than a tale of sponsorship, charter schools, and troubled communities. It is also a saga—sometimes a melodrama—of school reform in a key state in America's old industrial heartland, and in a once-proud city now buffeted by profound economic and social changes. Dayton and Ohio are struggling on multiple fronts, but nowhere more visibly than primary to secondary education. And nothing is more crucial to their revitalization than transforming the quality of their human capital, the performance of their schools, and the vitality of their neighborhoods.

Our story centers in those specific places, but it's not just about them. They are examples, representatives, illustrations—in today's vernacular one might say avatars—of far larger issues confronting America in the twenty-first century: issues of governmental competence and institutional effectiveness, of public and private interests, of economic renewal and international competitiveness, of social justice and equality of opportunity, and, of course, of the efficacy of academic standards and school choice as education renewal strategies.

A near-continuous thread in this story is the evolution of charter schooling in Ohio, home to four of the nation's top ten charter cities. In 2010, the Buckeye State had 330 charters serving more than 89,000 students. This form of school choice has been argued and fought over since its origins in 1997. Every year, more legislation has been proposed to reshape Ohio's charter program. Some measures would strengthen it, others stunt it. In 2009, as we wrote this book, Governor Ted Strickland sought to outlaw all forms of "for-profit" charter operators and cut funding for all charter schools. He was, for the time being, unsuccessful, but this remains a big and heated debate across Ohio, as it is across much of America.

Yet here, once again, something larger is at play. Clashes over charter schools are emblematic of the cosmic tussle between the established interests and institutional arrangements of public education, dominated by long-standing organizations and their ingrained priorities, and the forces of educational reform and renewal, largely dominated by families, elected officials, employers, and civic leaders. Can American primary and secondary education change to meet the demands that today's economy and society are placing upon it—or will it deflect such pressures and hew to its old ways?

The Fordham Institute has been in the midst of these debates nationally and in Ohio, with regard to both charter schools and the larger issues half-concealed in the background. Our story is informed by all these roles and it is one that we're pretty sure holds lessons for other education reformers. (In the concluding chapter, we share eighteen of the most important lessons we have distilled from our work in Ohio and beyond.)

Our recapitulation of what Fordham's experts learned when they went to school in Ohio helps to illumine the challenges of education reform in America, particularly urban America, and especially in the sphere of school choice. It describes the elements that we've found to be essential to high-performing schools and a system that sustains them. And it illustrates problems that remain to be solved and obstacles that still need to be surmounted for these and other education reforms to succeed in today's America.

Dayton and Columbus, Ohio
Washington, DC
February 2010

Notes

1. Erik W. Robelen, "A Think Tank Takes the Plunge," *Education Week*, December 20, 2006.
2. Dayton, Youngstown, Cleveland, and Toledo. See Todd Ziebarth, *Top 10 Charter Communities by Market Share* (Washington, DC: National Alliance for Public Charter Schools, 2008).

1

Dayton's Decline

Dayton is where Thomas B. Fordham made his fortune and where Chester Finn and Mike Lafferty grew up. Our roots there run deep. It's a city that was founded by frontiersmen and farmers at the confluence of three rivers in southwestern Ohio, but it became a model for early twentieth-century America at the hands of entrepreneurs, inventors, and businessmen. Tocqueville understood this spirit when he described Americans as being less interested in high-minded philosophy than in simply getting the job done. They want to grow it, make it better, and sell it for less than anyone else, he observed. Dayton typified this approach.

Indeed, Dayton typified much else. For decades it was a paradigmatic urban engine of America's industrial heartland. Its sturdy midwestern inhabitants were representative of what made the nation strong. When survey researcher Richard Scammon and social-political analyst Ben Wattenberg wrote *The Real Majority: An Extraordinary Examination of the American Electorate* in 1970, the suburban Dayton housewife was their most typical American.

Nevertheless, in the years that followed, Dayton went on to typify the nation's declining Rust Belt and its urban woes. That it also emerged as a hotbed of educational innovation—not all of it sound—is in large measure a response to the collapse of older civic, economic, and institutional arrangements that had once made it prosperous and strong.

Silicon Valley of the Midwest

The Wright brothers and their flying machines loom over Dayton's history, but the city has also spawned cash registers, refrigerators, automobile parts, aerospace technology, tires, paper, and many other products. John H. Patterson launched the National Cash Register (NCR) Company there in 1884, pioneering the practice of pleasant, well-lit working conditions for employees and a social welfare program that included an on-site doctor's office as well as other revolutionary concepts. For example, Patterson provided his workers chairs with backs instead of seating them on stools. He also produced a corps of trained executives who moved out from Dayton to lead businesses across the nation. One who started with Patterson was Charles F. Kettering, an inventor of the electric cash register. Kettering then founded, with Edward Deeds, the Dayton Electric Engineering Laboratories, where he developed the first electric starter for an automobile engine, as well as spark plugs and many other automotive devices. General Motors (GM) eventually purchased the company and renamed it Delco.

As much as anyone, Kettering was responsible for making Dayton one of the world's premier auto parts makers and appliance manufacturers in the twentieth century. Between the automotive and industrial engineers at the city's multiple GM plants, the fast-evolving office machines business at NCR, and the aerospace scientists at Wright Field, later Wright-Patterson Air Force Base, it's no exaggeration to say that, in the 1940s and 1950s, Dayton was the Silicon Valley of its day.

Abundant water and power, good schools, creative people, a central location, ample good transportation via road, rail, and air, and a highly skilled labor force made Dayton the third-largest employer of GM workers outside Detroit. Homes were purchased and families raised, especially in the two decades following World War II, fueled by a plethora of attractive jobs in the region's factories. "That's what you were expected to do, get a good factory job at Delco or Frigidaire," said Gary LeRoy, who grew up in the city during the 1960s and early 1970s.[1] Kathleen Stewart, the daughter of a Hungarian immigrant, felt lucky to live there and have a job at NCR. "All you had to do was grow up," she later recalled. "There was money everywhere."[2]

The principles of efficiency and innovation that defined Dayton's industry also took hold in its government, especially after the devastating flood of 1913 when the Great Miami River inundated downtown to the tops of the lampposts, destroying much of the city and killing 123 people. Led by Patterson, the community quickly organized recovery efforts and rebuilt itself (including a pioneering regional dam-and-flood-control system that has kept the city dry for nearly a century).[3] As part of that recovery, Patterson and other high-minded business and community leaders advanced the city manager style of government, a municipal reform arising from the progressive-era belief that people of vision, stature, objectivity, and competence should guide cities through elected commission members who then engaged a professional municipal manager—this in contrast to presumptively corrupt, nepotistic, and patronage-laden, mayor-controlled city halls. The commissioners would represent all the people by running "at large" and leading the community on behalf of their somewhat paternalistic understanding of the common good.

Patterson's group of good-government-minded civic leaders also looked after Dayton's schools. Just as city commission candidates were handpicked, wooed, and carefully vetted, so were candidates for the school board.[4] Once endorsed, they received powerful support in their campaigns. This father-knows-best approach to government worked satisfactorily so long as the business and economic machine ran smoothly. There was no need for messy, partisan political debate while the factories hummed and everyone saw the future as brighter than the present.

Industrialist Thomas B. Fordham was one of the community leaders who helped to guide Dayton during the first half of the twentieth century. Fordham, who managed the massive Frigidaire plant, was a local philanthropist and prominent civic figure until his death in 1944. His widow, the late Thelma Fordham Pruett, established the Thomas B. Fordham Foundation in his memory in 1959, and after she died in 1995, the foundation opted to focus its resources on the reform of primary and secondary education in Dayton and nationally. But that story comes later.

A Better Life for African Americans

Tens of thousands of African Americans migrated from the South to Dayton and other northern industrial cities, looking for jobs in factories and other businesses, especially during and after World War II. This influx changed the city's complexion from nearly 100 percent white to 30 percent black by the 1960s. But southwestern Ohio was not an altogether welcoming place for these new arrivals. Black Daytonians lived in separate neighborhoods near downtown or on the city's far west side and were largely invisible to whites. They faced de facto segregation and worse. The Ku Klux Klan had a strong presence in the region in the early twentieth century.

In 1921, the *Dayton Daily News* estimated area Klan membership at 15,000.[5] "In 1926," according to local historians Virginia and Bruce Ronald, "the Dayton Ku Klux Klan offered 40 Bibles to the new Daniel Kiser High School. The school board accepted, but noted that the Klan should not wear their white robes to the dedication of the building. They showed up in their robes and the school superintendent was in danger of losing his job because of the incident."[6]

Racial separation was so complete that Dayton became known as one of the most segregated cities in the United States, a circumstance that included its schools. Nevertheless, following Patterson's pragmatic, make-it-work philosophy, the city school board approached the job of educating black children much as it approached educating whites. Children of every hue needed schooling. But while black children needed to be educated *as well as* whites, they didn't need to be educated *with* whites and the school board steadfastly pursued "separate but equal."

For example, as noted in the 1977 federal court decision that imposed busing on Dayton, the district required "physical segregation into separate buildings of pupils and teachers by race at the Garfield School in the early 1920's, a denial to blacks of access to swimming pools in high schools in the 1930's and 1940's and the exclusion, between 1938 and 1948, of black high school teams from the city athletic conference."[7]

Roosevelt High School, which opened in 1927, was built strictly for black students, despite another high school just a mile away.[8] Dunbar High School—named after Dayton's most eminent black writer—was "established in 1933 as a black high school, taught by black teachers and attended by black pupils."[9] In 1969, the federal Office for Civil Rights reported that, among Dayton's 5,627 black high school students, 85 percent attended class in three of the city's eleven high schools, and about 85 percent of black elementary students attended twenty of the city's fifty-three elementary schools. In seventeen of those twenty, blacks made up 90 percent or more of the enrollment.[10]

For a time, separate-but-equal education fit Dayton's can-do philosophy. By the 1960s, though, as University of Dayton education analyst Joseph Watras argued in *Politics, Race and Schools: Racial Integration, 1954–1994,* Patterson's governance model was crumbling. The schools were especially troubled and were facing serious prointegration pressure from the city's black community as well as from Washington. Racial tensions were exacerbated by a faltering economy, which no longer generated the same wealth, jobs, and opportunity as it had.

In 1967, Richard Penry, then a young counselor at Colonel White High School on the city's northwest side, saw all of this firsthand. "When I started, the city schools were thriving as much as at any time," Penry recalls. "It was all about how many young people got into college. There was serious emphasis on the ACT and other college tests."[11]

Yet within four years of his arrival the nearly all white student body at Colonel White had become 25 percent black. As part of the tumultuous 1960s, African Americans had asserted their right to work, live, and vote where they wanted and started moving across Wolf Creek from their traditional neighborhoods into the established white areas of Dayton View. That migration created tensions and spawned gangs, both black and white. Ohio National Guard troops quelled racial disturbances in the city during the summer of 1967, concurrent with race riots in other U.S. cities.

At Colonel White, teachers and administrators tried to keep a lid on the volatile mix of ethnic tensions, teenage hormones, and political passions. Still, Penry says, students continued to receive a decent education while the high school's faculty remained stable and able. But that didn't last long. When Penry returned as principal to Colonel White in 1995, the school bore little resemblance to the educational institution he had left two decades earlier. The urban problems he had read about in major metro areas now swarmed the corridors outside his office. There were attendance challenges, drugs, and violence. Metal detectors had been installed at the main entrance and academic performance had collapsed.[12]

Tim Nealon started working in Dayton in 1967 as a teacher at Dunbar High School. (Five years later, he transferred to Colonel White where he eventually served as assistant principal under Penry.) Nealon, who grew up in Dayton, started teaching at Dunbar soon after that school was rocked by what he recalled as a "mini-riot." Like many whites, Nealon had never thought much about segregation in the city. "The troubles in the late 1960s scared the community. Nobody had a clue," he recalled during an interview for this book. "The economics and poverty and everything falling apart [were] swept under the rug." Arriving at Dunbar as a neophyte English instructor, Nealon was one of about ten white teachers in a nearly all black school.

Like Roosevelt, Dunbar was constructed as part of the Dayton public schools' separate-but-equal planning. Everything was first class, including the black teaching staff. "That was one of the most powerful groups of teachers I ever worked with," Nealon recollects. "A lot were nearing retirement. They were good teachers, good, old-school—the 'keep your nose in the books and your feet to the fire' kind."[13]

Dunbar strove to meet the needs of its pupils and community. "Those teachers knew the kids and their parents," says Nealon. "The parents probably had the same teachers when they were kids." Yet "all hell broke loose" in 1969 through 1970. Dayton schools were consumed in the larger racial tensions burning across the nation. What Nealon termed "outside agitators" tried to shut down Dunbar by setting it on fire or entering the building to disrupt classes. "A [black] guy came down the hall one day," Nealon said. "He had a shotgun and he held [it] on me."[14]

Nealon fled into his classroom with his students and locked the door but the man knocked out the glass in the door with the gun and stuck the barrel into the room, demanding that teacher and pupils leave. "It was total chaos at that point. There was little going on in terms of education. Everyone in the school had become supersensitive and when [school superintendent] Wayne Carle tried to create a black culture course for the curriculum there was an explosive backlash."[15]

Because the school system was encountering difficulty finding replacements for retiring administrators, Nealon, after just three years of teaching, was promoted to administration. In 1971, he was assistant principal at Dunbar. "They couldn't find a [more experienced] white guy to go into the school as an administrator," he said. "It was not untypical to have herds of kids running down the hall at the drop of a hat." Students had got hold of a set of the custodian's keys so the school was wide open to vandalism and chaos. Almost daily, someone would set fire to the stage curtain in the school auditorium. The fires became a sort of running joke. "The first day on the job I was [accidentally] hosed down by these kids trying to put the fire out," he said. The curtains were not actually flammable but they singed and melted a little, day after day, for months.[16]

Gary LeRoy's mother was one of thousands of African Americans who came to Dayton in the years after World War II. She migrated from Greenville, Mississippi, and, once in Dayton, worked in a variety of low-paying jobs, finally settling as a domestic worker earning about $60 a week. She was among the first wave of black Daytonians to move into a predominantly white neighborhood in lower Dayton View, where LeRoy, now a doctor, still lives. White or black, economics bound the neighborhood together: everyone was poor. Still, it was a step up for the LeRoys. It was his mother's first house and they were the second black family on Williams Street. At the time, LeRoy recalled, people mostly got along. Gradually more black families moved in and more white families moved out.[17]

LeRoy said he didn't meet real prejudice until he went to high school. "When I went to Colonel White, I wondered, 'Why do these [white] people hate us so much?' These people didn't know me from Adam. I had never met them." For the most part he did not remember prejudice affecting his education. "I thought I had a good education until someone told me I hadn't," he said. "My purpose was to go to school, to get good grades, not mediocre grades but good grades. Mediocre grades would have disappointed my mother who was working so hard to put me there."[18]

LeRoy credits his success to good teachers, black and white, who saw his potential and encouraged it. He is now medical director of the East Dayton Health Center, holds an appointment at Wright State University, and is chief medical consultant to the Dayton public schools. His success is far from unique, but it is a trajectory that few of the city's black students are on today. LeRoy says the district has a tough job dealing with students who start off school so far behind their more fortunate peers. He suggests that poor test scores reflect the lack of jobs and hope, as well as poor health and nutrition in families. These problems, if you looked, would parallel poor test scores everywhere. "It's like a big negative feedback loop," Dr. LeRoy said. "If you're not healthy, you can't go to school."[19]

Busing and Its Aftermath

While Colonel White became biracial, that wasn't true of the Dayton public schools as a whole. As in many cities, the federal government was increasing pressure on the district to integrate its schools, but in view of continuing residential separation the only way that could happen was through busing. It was just a matter of time before a federal judge, in this case district judge Carl Rubin, ordered the district, in 1976, to begin transporting its pupils across town. He held that "the 'great majority' of the 66 schools were imbalanced and that, with one exception [Colonel White], the Dayton School Board had made no affirmative effort to achieve racial balance within those schools."[20]

His decision was appealed all the way to the United States Supreme Court, which in June 1977 ruled that the Dayton Board of Education had indeed denied the "constitutional guarantee of equal protection of the laws in a northern city where state law did not mandate a dual school system."[21] The Supreme Court upheld the sixth circuit's earlier ruling that "the racial composition of each school in the district [must] be brought within 15% of Dayton's 48%–52% black-white population ratio, to be accompanied by a variety of desegregation techniques." Such techniques included the "transportation of approximately 15,000 students on a regular and permanent basis."[22]

Earlier attempts by the school board to avoid legal action and proactively address desegregation had been met with a backlash that saw supporters of an all-white antibusing group eventually gain control of the board. This group put pressure on Superintendent Carle—who had mounted a strong push for integration and for getting blacks and whites to work together around the schools—to scrap all such plans.[23] His opponents insisted that children go to neighborhood schools, segregated or not. This meant, in practice, that—until the courts decreed otherwise—the district would remain racially divided since, except for lower Dayton View, there were almost no mixed residential areas in the city.

The move by Judge Rubin and those above him to force Dayton to join Chicago, Boston, Cleveland, Columbus, and many other cities in busing children for purposes of racial balance triggered anger and mistrust that would roil the Dayton public schools into the twenty-first century. Dr. LeRoy is one of many Daytonians who blame busing for precipitating white flight to the suburbs and ultimately bleeding Dayton of its middle class, wrecking neighborhoods and devastating the city's public school system. "We destroyed the community school concept by busing children all over kingdom come," LeRoy said. "Dayton was one of the last cities in the country to give up compulsory busing [in 2002]. So many whites had fled the city for economic reasons and because they hated busing."[24]

Former *Dayton Daily News* education reporter Mark Fisher declares that the all-white school board brought many of the ensuing problems upon itself. "The desegregation order was earned by the processes the school district employed prior to the order coming down," he said in an interview for this book. "They thumbed their nose at the process . . . at plaintiffs, the process and the federal court."[25] The anti-integrationists ultimately lost the battle, but not before it scarred the city and spawned the murder, in 1975, of Ohio State University professor Charles Glatt, who was appointed by the court to develop a busing plan. Glatt was shot to death in his office in Dayton's downtown federal building by Neal Bradley Long, who was subsequently linked to at least seven racially motivated murders and ultimately sentenced to two consecutive terms of life imprisonment.

Fisher agrees with LeRoy and others that busing destroyed the concept of neighborhood schools and that this contributed greatly to Dayton's decline. Although white flight was under way in the 1960s, Fisher says the desegregation order accelerated it. Some of those who left from 1972 to 1975 fled in anticipation that such a court order was imminent, he believes. Once busing actually began, though, it became evident how important neighborhood schools were, and not least to black Daytonians. "Neighborhood schools generated stronger attachment and a stronger sense of pride," Fisher said, arguing that "forcibly" removing children from their neighborhoods, subjecting them to bus rides of up to forty-five minutes each way, making them wait for buses in the dark, and sometimes not getting them home until after dark, soured public opinion. "You had marching bands with 120 kids and five years [later] maybe they had 20 members," Fisher said, citing both Dunbar, a still mostly black high school on the West Side, and Belmont, a mostly white school on the East Side.

Busing also affected parents' support for their kids' schools as it grew more difficult for them to get to school events, PTA meetings, and the like. "A lot of people who lived near Belmont High School moved to the suburbs," Fisher recalls. "It was people who could afford to move, people involved with the education of their children who moved." The result, he argues, was devastating. "[That] took the top 20%. . . . when you skim the top 20%, I think you have more than a 20% impact. Students lose their role models, teachers lose hope."[26]

By 2001, after twenty-four years of busing and its side effects, most Daytonians, black and white, had had enough. A *Dayton Daily News* survey of 600 residents indicated that more than 53 percent of black parents believed busing for desegregation should end, while only 34 percent wanted it to continue. The same survey showed 80 percent of parents grading the

Dayton public schools C or below. Sixty-one percent said they would send their children to private schools if they could afford it. Erosion in confidence was greatest among black parents. Fifteen years earlier, in 1986, a similar survey had shown more than half of black parents giving an A or B grade to the district. In 2001, fewer than 25 percent did so.[27]

Issues of race defined school politics in Dayton on into the twenty-first century. Starting in the 1960s, the Dayton public schools (DPS) produced a succession of short-term superintendents, bitter school board clashes, and lasting community divisions, which spilled over into failed efforts to pass tax levies to enable the district to make financial ends meet. In 2007, for example, the DPS failed to pass an operating levy by a 58 to 42 percent vote. The city's East Side, primarily white and Appalachian, voted overwhelmingly against it, while the West Side, still almost wholly African American, voted for it, with support between 60 and 70 percent in most neighborhoods.

When federal district judge Walter H. Rice ended busing in 2002, the city schools were 70 percent black.[28]

Economic Meltdown

Achievement in Dayton's public schools was faltering even before the National Commission on Excellence in Education declared in 1983 that the future prosperity and security of the entire country were at risk due to the weak performance of its education system. But Dayton's situation went from bad to worse. A 1994 Phi Delta Kappa study slammed the district for failing to boost academic performance.

That report was scathing, declaring that teachers did not teach, or at best taught poorly. They did not receive quality training or feedback from district officials. And despite eight major district improvement plans between 1984 and 1994, the Phi Delta Kappa analysts found little evidence that the school board or administrators had actually implemented any of the changes.[29]

Since at least the 1980s, the district has constantly struggled to attain basic educational standards. By the 1990s, DPS was battling Cleveland for the dubious distinction of being the state's worst performing system. In 2002, the Council of the Great City Schools captured the scale of the academic problems facing the city's schools when it observed that "no urban school system in Ohio has fewer children meeting state proficiency standards. Only 23% of Dayton Public School fourth graders met state reading benchmarks in 2000, compared with 34% in Cleveland, 35% in Toledo,

37% in Columbus and 29% in Cincinnati. Math scores are worse. The problem appears to be exacerbated by high teacher absenteeism."[30]

While its schools struggled to educate the city's ever-poorer children, Dayton saw its middle-class economy dismantled and outsourced. Since the 1970s, the city has lost tens of thousands of manufacturing jobs as well as thousands of positions in support industries, especially the once booming tool-and-die industry, even though the overall U.S. economy grew at a healthy pace for most of this period.

First very gradually, then faster, factories laid off workers, cut back operations, and finally closed. The firms that had made Dayton the "Gem City" in the first half of the twentieth century led the way to the exits. Every year brought a new round of layoffs and plant closings. Manufacturing employment in the metro area dropped 30 percent during the 1970s.[31]

"If we had grown at the rate of the national economy during this time, we would have added 100,000 new jobs," said Dayton city economist Diane Shannon. "There's a clear indication that people were not moving to Dayton well before the problems with the schools."[32]

Economic and employment data have not stopped their deterioration. From 2000 to 2008, jobs in the Dayton metro area dropped eight percent even as they increased in Ohio by 2.5 percent and in the nation by five percent.[33] The last half of 2008 and early 2009 were particularly brutal. In August 2009, unemployment across the United States was 9.7 percent, but in Ohio it was 10.8 percent and in Dayton 12.9 percent.[34] These numbers were for adults actively looking for work and would be even grimmer if they included the many Dayton adults who had given up looking for legitimate employment or those who simply left the city looking for opportunity elsewhere.

As their jobs vanished and schools declined, people exited the community. Dayton's population, which peaked at about 262,000 in 1960, was down to 182,044 by 1990 and to 143,974 in 2008.[35] Between 1970 and 2000, the city lost nearly a third of its population, although the county remained relatively stable (see Table 1.1).

In late 2007, the *Columbus Dispatch* summed up Dayton's decline in these bleak terms: "North Main Street is an eerie ghost town of boarded-up buildings and vacant lots, poverty rates are skyrocketing and mortgage foreclosures are pushing Dayton residents out of the American dream. Blight is rooted in some parts of the city. One weed-clogged neighborhood gas station has been closed so long that the price on the sign says it all: 86.9 cents per gallon."[36]

Those who remain in the city are increasingly poor. According to census figures, Dayton ranked as the ninth poorest medium-sized city in the United States in 2005. Fully 29 percent of its residents had incomes below

Table 1.1   Population, Dayton and Montgomery County

Date	City of Dayton	Montgomery County	Dayton as % of Montgomery County
1970	262,332	608,413	43.1
1980	243,023	571,100	42.5
1990	182,044	573,809	31.7
2000	166,179	559,062	29.7
2007 est.	146,762	541,502	27.1
2008 est.	143,974	534,626	26.9

Sources: U.S. Census Bureau, 1990, 2000, American Community Survey 2005–2007, 2008; Ohio Department of Development, Decennial Census of Population, by county 1800–2000 (http://www.development.ohio.gov/research/FILES/P009110001.pdf), by place 1900–2000 (http://www.development.ohio.gov/research/FILES/P009110003.pdf).

the poverty level in 2008, more than double the Ohio average.[37] Close to 90 percent of children attending the Dayton public schools are poor enough to qualify for a free or reduced-price lunch.[38]

Yet these numbers, alarming as they are, don't tell the full story. Dayton has also lost many of its best and brightest. High school and college graduates left town, never to return. "There wasn't anything to come back to," Penry said. "The drain of talent started way back in the 1970s."[39] Some people left the whole midwestern region for jobs in burgeoning southern and southwestern states. But the goal of many others was simply to move to the suburbs, which continued to grow throughout the second half of the twentieth century and into the twenty-first.

The suburbs got their start by absorbing the spillover from the City of Dayton during World War II, when an estimated 100,000 people arrived there to work in the then-booming factories and defense plants. After the war, these workers remained and found jobs at NCR, General Motors, Dayton Tire and Rubber, McCall's, and hundreds of other thriving firms. The city could not absorb so many new residents, so thousands settled in Fairborn, Kettering, Beavercreek, Trotwood, and other nearby towns.

Dayton's was, in some ways, the classic postwar tale of American cities. As the suburbs boomed with newcomers, infrastructure and services followed, and, once there were roads, sewers, schools, and affordable housing, longtime urban residents also began to move outward.[40] The growth of the suburbs corresponded with Dayton's long-standing but short-sighted policy of not annexing adjacent territory.

Despite suggestions to the contrary, in an effort to concentrate develop-ment in Dayton, municipal leaders generally refused to add acreage to the city itself, which policy backfired by cutting Dayton off from the region's rapid economic and population growth.[41] Suburbs like Kettering and Bea-vercreek continued to expand into the 1980s and 1990s, not so much as a result of in-migration to the region as of people moving out of Dayton. While the Miami Valley region has struggled economically and demograph-ically, Dayton has had it worse (see Table 1.2). The city's median household income in 2007 was 30 percent less than in 1970. Former school board member Susan Stibbing believes that Daytonians moved away because they feared falling housing values and worried that the schools were going to get worse. "It got so bad by the [1980s]," she said, "that the city passed a resi-dency requirement for managers, firefighters and police." (To the dismay of city leaders, in June 2009 the Ohio Supreme Court upheld a state law that prohibited such restrictions.) No one moved into the city. "It wasn't that people just moved [out]," Stibbing explains. "The houses they had lived in became rentals or went vacant."[42] In 2008, *Forbes* magazine rated Dayton as being the "fifth emptiest city" in America.[43]

As this book was being completed, Dayton learned that both the Iams Pet Food Company, owned by Proctor and Gamble, and the NCR Corpora-tion were moving out of the city and taking more than 1,500 middle-class jobs with them. The NCR move was especially painful because this was the company that John Patterson had built and it had been a part of Dayton's

Table 1.2   Poverty rate and median household income (in constant 2007 dollars), Dayton and Montgomery County

Date	*Poverty rate (%)*		*Median household income (2007 dollars)*	
	City	County	City ($)	County ($)
1970	14.2	8.2	56,493.25*	67,162.24
1980	20.0	11.0	36,131.67	52,451.31
1990	25.5	11.8	34,448.80	52,443.89
2000	23.0	11.3	35,549.33	50,362.67
2007 est.	29.6	14.8	29,561.86	45,967.18
2008 est.	29.2	15.1	29,605.30	56,641.67

Sources: U.S. Census Bureau, American Community Survey 2005–7 (3-year estimates), ACS 2008 estimates; Ohio Department of Development, Bureau of Labor Statistics CPI inflation calculator.
*Data reflects Dayton standard metropolitan statistical area of the 1970 census.

community fabric for 125 years. It was Dayton's last Fortune 500 company and at its peak in the 1950s it employed 20,000 area workers. "Perhaps because of its history of paternalism here, the company's leaving is a little like losing a parent,"[44] Susan Toole, a Dayton area clinical psychologist told the *Dayton Daily News*.[45] Or, as the vice president of the Dayton Development Coalition said, "This is definitely the big one—the most painful one to lose."[46]

The *New York Times* summarized the situation facing Dayton in late June 2009. According to the article, the city faced a vortex of "economic and social change. The area's job total has fallen 12% since 2000, while about half of its factory jobs—38,000 out of 79,000—have disappeared this decade. Not only have large G.M. and Delphi plants closed, but NCR, long the city's corporate jewel, recently announced that it would move its headquarters to the Atlanta area."[47]

Dayton Public Schools

By 2009, DPS served barely fifteen thousand students: less than a third of the system's peak (1965) enrollment. Despite this hemorrhaging, over the decades officials largely continued to operate the school system as if little had changed. For too long, they did not redesign or rightsize the district's basic financial or program structures, or make a systematic effort to compete with private, parochial, charter, and suburban schools. Education analyst Paul Hill argues that DPS was able to deal with decline for much of this period without too much pain by simply shrinking its workforce through attrition.[48] The district contracted by not hiring new teachers as older instructors retired.

In more recent years cost cutting has meant layoffs. Because state law, pushed through by the teacher unions, requires the last hired to be the first fired, the younger and less-expensive teachers must depart, and with them goes their energy and the district's future labor force. In 2007, Dayton's "Teacher of the Year" was given that award with one hand and his layoff notice with the other.

James Williams may have had the last best chance to turn the district in the right direction when he was elevated from assistant superintendent to superintendent in 1991. "Parents were tired of failing schools and they were looking for a solution," Williams said in an interview for this book. He planned to work with a broad coalition of community leaders to convert five failing schools into district-sponsored charter schools in 1997. At this time, charter schools were a brand new concept in Ohio. Williams envisioned educational "high-flyers" with innovative teaching programs, longer days, and a longer school year designed to boost student achievement. He dreamed of someday converting the entire district to charters. Ultimately, Williams couldn't get even his five-school pilot off the ground. (This sad tale is recounted in Chapter 3.) That idea engendered such strong union disapproval that Williams was unable to get it past his own board. "It was the biggest disappointment in my career," said Williams, who is now superintendent in Buffalo. He declared, in 2008, "Dayton, you have lost an opportunity. This town is going to die. You have lost an opportunity to control the situation. This town is going to die."[49]

A casual visitor might agree. A trip through today's Dayton reveals its fraying municipal threads. Once the shopping magnet of several counties, Dayton's downtown is now a shadow of its former self, having lost all its upscale retail to the suburbs and their malls. There's little new development. Activity is centered on government buildings and a few high-rise office buildings, often with occupancy levels below 70 percent. Downtown is forlorn even by day. To be fair, many American downtowns, particularly in the old industrial heartland, have a similar feel in the evenings. There's not much going on in downtown Columbus after dark. Yet Columbus and even downtown Cleveland evince energy by day, and there's obvious ongoing investment and development.

As is the case for America as a whole, only more so in the Midwest, any revival for a city like Dayton will depend in no small part on its schools. Community leaders see education as critical to reconstituting the city as a livable place for middle-class families. They have repeatedly called for more academic rigor, greater customer focus, and more effort at rightsizing district operations. Yet their "pleas all too often fell on deaf ears," said Ron Budzik, a retired Mead executive who has been actively involved in Dayton education issues for decades. In the 1990s and early 2000s, he explains, "The board and superintendent acknowledged that something should be done but seemed to not [actually] want to do anything." Their attitude was, "We're the pros, we don't need any help."[50]

Other cities in the region faced similar challenges, a fact captured in 2007 by Mayor Frank Jackson of Cleveland when he told the *Columbus Dispatch*, "Our problem is families with children. People are making their choices based on education, and if I am able to make our school district a district of choice where people want to put their children because of excellence, then I can guarantee you that our population reduction will come to a halt."[51] For Dayton and kindred communities, when it comes to education, the stakes are huge and the cost of continued failure is incalculable.

Notes

1. Gary LeRoy, interview by Mike Lafferty, January 29, 2008.
2. Quoted in Sara Rimer, "A Hometown Feels Less Like Home," *New York Times*, March 6, 1996, http://www.nytimes.com/1996/03/06/us/a-hometown -feels-less-like-home.html?scp=1&sq=a%20hometown%20feels%20less %20like%20home&st=cse.
3. Virginia Ronald and Bruce Ronald, *The Lands between the Miamis: A Bicentennial Celebration of the Dayton Area* (Dayton, OH: Landfall Press, 1996), 259. For more on the history of the Great Flood of 1913 and its aftermath, see http://www.miamiconservancy.org/about/history.asp.
4. Joseph Watras, *Politics, Race and Schools: Racial Integration, 1954–1994* (New York: Garland, 1997), xiii.
5. Ronald and Ronald, *Lands between the Miamis*, 289.
6. Ibid.
7. *Dayton Board of Education et al., Petitioners v. Mark Brinkman et al.*, 433 U.S. 406 (1977).
8. Interviews by Michael Lafferty with Tim Nealon, February 2008; Joseph Watras, February 21, 2008; and Richard Penry, January 17, 2008.
9. *Dayton Board of Education*, 433 U.S. 406.
10. Mark Fisher and Scott Elliott, "Poll: Many Black Parents against Busing Program," *Dayton Daily News*, May 20, 2001, 1A.
11. Penry, interview.
12. Ibid.
13. Nealon, interview.
14. Ibid.
15. Ibid.
16. Ibid.
17. LeRoy, interview.
18. Ibid.
19. Ibid.
20. *Dayton Board of Education*, 433 U.S. 406.
21. Morton Mintz, "School Bias Remedy Must Fit Offense; Remedy for School Bias Must Fit Violation; Court Rule Unanimous," *Washington Post*, June 28, 1977, A1.
22. *Dayton Board of Education*, 433 U.S. 406.
23. Watras, *Politics, Race and Schools*.
24. LeRoy, interview.
25. Mark Fisher, interview by Mike Lafferty, February 21, 2008.
26. Ibid.
27. Scott Elliott and Mark Fisher, "Faith in Schools Falling," *Dayton Daily News*, May 24, 2001, 1A.
28. Ohio Department of Education, *2002–3 School Year Report Card: Dayton City District*, http://www.ode.state.oh.us/reportcardfiles/2002-2003/DIST/ 043844.pdf.

29. Phi Delta Kappa Study of Dayton City School District, Dayton, OH, 1994.
30. *Raising Student Achievement in the Dayton Public Schools*, Council of the Great City Schools, Washington, DC, February 2002, 11.
31. Jon C. Teaford, *Cities of the Heartland: The Rise and Fall of the Industrial Midwest* (Bloomington: Indiana University Press, 1993), 221.
32. Diane Shannon, interview by Mike Lafferty, January 28, 2008.
33. Richard Stock, Business Research Group, University of Dayton, Dayton, OH, 2008.
34. Ohio Department of Jobs and Family Services, *Current Labor Force Estimates*, January 2009, http://lmi.state.oh.us/laus/current.htm.
35. Ohio Department of Development, *Decennial Census of Population, 1900 to 2000, by Place*, March 2001, 8, http://nodisnet1.csuohio.edu/nodis/historic/pop_place19002000.pdf; U.S. Census Bureau American Fact Finder, *Dayton City, OH*, 2005–2007, http://factfinder.census.gov/servlet/ADPTable?_bm=y&-geo_id=16000US3921000&-qr_name=ACS_2007_3YR_G00_DP3YR5&-ds_name=ACS_2007_3YR_G00_&-_lang=en&-_sse=on.
36. Alan Johnson, "On the Brink: Dayton," *Columbus Dispatch*, December 4, 2007, http://www.dispatch.com/live/content/local_news/stories/2007/12/04/DAYTON.ART_ART_12-04-07_A1_K18KVSU.html?sid=101.
37. Ohio Department of Development, *Decennial Census of Population*.
38. *Next Steps in the Improvement of the Dayton Public Schools*, Report of the Strategic Support Team of the Council of the Great City Schools, Washington, DC, Fall 2008, 16.
39. Penry, interview.
40. Shannon, interview, 2008.
41. Ibid.; Nealon, interview, January 30, 2008.
42. Susan Stibbing, interview by Mike Lafferty, January 2008.
43. Joshua Zumbrun, "America's Fastest-Dying Cities," *Forbes*, August 5, 2008, http://www.forbes.com/2008/08/04/economy-ohio-michigan-biz_cx_jz_0805dying.html.
44. Jim DeBrosse and Jessica Wehrman, "Recovery Won't Be Easy: NCR's Leaders Once Fought Dayton's Battles Large and Small," *Dayton Daily News*, June 3, 2009, A4.
45. Ibid.
46. Ibid.
47. Steven Greenhouse, "As Plants Close, Teenagers Focus More on College," *New York Times*, June 26, 2009.
48. Paul Hill, *Learning As We Go: Why School Choice is Worth the Wait* (Stanford, CA: Hoover Institution Press, 2010), 44.
49. James Williams, interview by Mike Lafferty, April 2008.
50. Ron Budzik, interview by Mike Lafferty, June 12, 2008.
51. Mark Niquette, Alan Johnson, and Joe Hallett, "On the Brink: Can Ohio's Big Cities Be Saved?" *Columbus Dispatch*, December 2, 2007, http://www.dispatch.com/live/content/special_reports/stories/2007/cities/index.html.

2

The Dawn of Charter Schools

To make sense of the complex origins of Ohio's charter school program and related school and school finance reforms, it helps to understand the state and its political divisions, some of America's most distinctive. These divisions turn out to be more complicated than big-city Democrats versus suburban and rural Republicans. Few other states have eight major cities. Known, in fact, as the Big 8, they marked Ohio politics throughout the twentieth century. Other states have regional competitions: New York City versus upstate, Chicago versus downstate, northern versus southern California, and so forth. What makes Ohio different, explains political scientist Herb Asher, who has studied Buckeye State politics for decades, is that, except for the thinly populated semi-Appalachian southeast, every region of Ohio has a major population center that generates parochial demands and political power.

These competing "city-states," electing lawmakers looking to boost their hometowns, have balkanized Ohio. For many years, that was also true of the state's economy, as each region developed its own manufacturing base, save for Columbus, whose economy has always depended more on government, higher education, research, and insurance. Cleveland and Youngstown had steel; Cincinnati, machinery; Toledo, glass and autos; Akron and Canton, rubber and ball bearings; and Dayton, auto parts and home appliances. In a medium-sized state with—in recent years—a flat population and static economy, this made for vicious competition for development funding and much else. Besides one-on-one rivalries, cities form cliques. Akron, Canton, Dayton, Toledo, and Youngstown have often been pitted against the "Three Cs"—Cleveland, Columbus, and Cincinnati—for what they view as their fair share of state and federal dollars.

Regional competition plays out prominently in legislative tussles over highway dollars and state subsidies to attract industry or build sports arenas. There's chronic resentment in central, southern, and western Ohio toward the populous northeastern part of the state. And, at one time or another, each of the other seven has envied Columbus. A perennial lament, for example, is that Ohio State University is protected at the expense of other state colleges and universities. To assuage northeastern worries that too much government money was going to Columbus, the state established a large state government complex in Cleveland, basically a second administrative center. The Ohio Lottery Commission, for example, is based in Cleveland.

Education Dollars and the DeRolph Case

One result of this municipal and regional competition is that Ohio has established fourteen state universities with twenty-four branch campuses, as well as twenty-three community colleges. The state also boasts more than 50 private institutions of higher learning, which vie with state schools for students, resources, and prestige.[1] "We have six public medical schools in the state," Asher noted in an interview for this book. "Six public medical schools are a lot. That is probably a reflection that medical schools are important and that each region would like to have access to one."[2]

Because towns and cities run their own school systems, school issues can be especially divisive—and never more so than the spending of state tax dollars on public education. Through much of the twentieth century Ohio used a funding model devised in the 1930s. By the mid-1970s, that distribution scheme was revealing serious failings, notably its inability to account for disparities in income and property tax wealth between rich and poor districts at a time of mounting zeal for educational equality.

School funding became a highly charged political issue, especially after the General Assembly barred districts in 1976 from automatically collecting more taxes as inflation pushed up property values. That change made taxing for education more democratic and populist, since districts now needed voter approval to pass periodic school levies. But it also forced school officials to go to the local electorate every few years in search of resources. The double whammy of rising education costs and declining industry played havoc with urban districts and their ability to raise what they regarded as enough money for their schools. In consequence, Ohio's urban and rural schools fell further behind their better-heeled suburban counterparts.

In dozens of states, these issues of equity and adequacy in education funding moved from the statehouse to the courtroom as litigants, advocacy groups, and attorneys sought—with considerable success—to have judges mandate fundamental overhauls of traditional distribution formulas. For

Ohio, this saga commenced in 1991 when a fifteen-year-old student at Sheridan High School in rural Perry County agreed to serve as guinea pig in a lawsuit against the state for not providing his school district with enough money for an adequate education. What became known as the "DeRolph case" was born when Nathan DeRolph, his father, and five school districts asked Common Pleas judge Linton Lewis to declare the state's education funding mechanism unconstitutional.

Every Ohio child, they contended, had a constitutional right to a good education no matter where he or she resided. Perry County and other rural districts had large amounts of low-tax-producing farmland. There was no way they could support their schools at the same level as, say, the rich Columbus suburb of Worthington. The lawsuit contended that the state wasn't doing enough to reduce disparities between what local taxpayers could afford to pay and what was needed for a good education. Eventually, 550 school districts joined the case, represented by an umbrella group calling itself the Coalition for Equity and Adequacy of School Funding.

In 1994, Judge Lewis ruled that Ohio's school funding system was indeed unconstitutional. The state appealed and, eventually, the case reached the Ohio Supreme Court. On March 24, 1997, the court agreed with Lewis and gave the governor and general assembly one year to overhaul the school finance system. Although Governor George Voinovich and GOP legislative leaders blasted the justices and threatened to defy their decision,[3] they nevertheless in time went to work injecting more state dollars into schools and districts. The supreme court watched all this closely, as did the Coalition for Equity and Adequacy. In 2000 and twice more in 2001 the justices ruled that school funding still depended overmuch on local property taxes and thereby perpetuated unacceptable inequities across districts.

In 2001, one frustrated justice actually wanted to shut down the state government until the legislature complied with the court's order to fix the system. Another thought the court might have to order the arrest of the new governor and members of the general assembly. "We were coming very close to the only thing left was to put [Governor Bob] Taft in jail, or the General Assembly in jail," said Justice Andy Douglas, a populist Republican who led the court's series of narrow four-to-three DeRolph verdicts. In time, though, the court took a step back. In 2001 it held that the state's school funding system was unconstitutional, and it ordered the state to alter its funding methodology for determining the per-pupil base support and to accelerate the phase-in of parity aid, "at which point" the court said, "the system will be constitutional."[4]

On May 16, 2003, the Ohio Supreme Court stated that "we now grant a preemptory writ and end any further *DeRolph* litigation in *DeRolph v. State*."[5] An appeal to the United States Supreme Court was denied in

October 2003. Republican lawmakers and the governor declared victory. "The DeRolph case is over," Taft announced after the court's dismissal.[6] Many others, including the Coalition for Equity and Adequacy and a number of Democratic lawmakers, were frustrated, but the case, at least in the courts, was concluded.[7]

Urban School Meltdown: Cleveland and Beyond

The arrival of charter schools in Ohio was a subplot of this larger fiscal, political, and education policy drama. The state's initial charter law (1997) coincided almost exactly with the supreme court's first DeRolph decision. Although the *Columbus Dispatch* pilloried that ruling as "one of the most-poorly reasoned, overreaching decisions to emanate from the high court in a long time,"[8] it would have a profound impact on the charter school debate—and much else—for more than a decade. School funding and charters would always be seen as interconnected by opponents of the latter.

But, of course, that's not the full story. By the time of the DeRolph case, serious angst could be discerned in many quarters regarding the fiscal and academic performance of Ohio's urban districts. Cleveland and Dayton were both educational basket cases and Cleveland was literally on the brink of bankruptcy. In 1995, its schools faced a $160 million debt—about a third of the system's operating budget. Conditions were so dire that a federal judge ordered the state superintendent of education to take over district operations. But the GOP-led state legislature wanted to know exactly what it was getting into, and in the 1995 budget bill ordered State Auditor Jim Petro to perform a thorough audit of the Cleveland schools.[9]

At $700,000, this was the most expensive and extensive performance audit of a public school system conducted in the United States to that time, and, when it was released on March 15, 1996, it hit both district and legislators like a tornado. The Cleveland Public Schools were effectively broke, both academically and financially. Technically, school districts can't declare bankruptcy, like private companies, but Petro used the analogy because it fit so well. "I think by any definition of bankruptcy as we know it with a private business, they've got some serious problems," he said. "They would be deemed bankrupt."[10]

Cleveland's predicament was especially galling to suburban and rural Republicans because the audit showed that, although insolvent, the Cleveland Public Schools were largely on the state dole and asking for even more money via the DeRolph lawsuit. In 1997, local taxes paid for just 31 percent of the cost of Cleveland's schools compared with a statewide average of 51 percent.[11] Nor were profound fiscal challenges confined to Cleveland. The

Dispatch, for example, reported that "many facets of the Columbus school system, including staffing, salaries and the ratio of school buildings to students, resemble Cleveland's bankrupt schools."[12] Dayton faced similar fiscal problems even as new, state-mandated report cards were beginning to reveal the academic performance of these districts to be just as troubled.

While often embarrassing, especially to urban districts, these report cards, which first appeared in 1998, have proved invaluable in aiding voters and taxpayers to gauge the performance of their schools. Until Ohio developed these educational performance dashboards, citizens had no real way of knowing how their schools were doing or how they compared with each other. Further, the revelation—via state tests—of just how poorly big-city districts were performing proved crucial to the push to create charter schools and widen other forms of education choice. Critics now had irrefutable evidence of systematic and repeated educational failure, not just anecdotes. And these hard data made it easier for choice proponents to argue that students should not remain trapped in sorely troubled schools where—it was now evident—they learned little.

Bad news from the state's major urban districts triggered a strong reaction at the statehouse. Then-chairman of the House Education Committee, GOP legislator Michael A. Fox reflected the views of many in his party when he declared that the schools were in dire shape. "To invest more money in these failed systems without making a fundamental structural change in the way these schools do business will not help children," he asserted in 1996.[13] It was time "to recognize that our urban districts have performed so poorly that they have forfeited their right to hold the franchise on providing education to Ohio's urban school children."[14] Representative Jim Jordan, a Republican from the small town of West Liberty, was terser: "The people of my area are tired of supporting a 34% graduation rate in Cleveland."[15]

Vouchers for Cleveland

With abysmal state academic data, low graduation rates, and other headline-grabbing problems, the stage was set to give students and parents some alternatives. School choice first raised its head in Ohio as early as 1992 when Governor Voinovich—a former mayor of Cleveland—created the Governor's Commission on Educational Choice and appointed Akron industrialist and longtime Republican activist David Brennan to chair it. Brennan would play a pivotal role in the creation of the Cleveland voucher program (officially the "Cleveland Scholarship and Tutoring Program"), then a hugely controversial role in the state's fledgling charter school program. As its name implied, the commission's mandate was to develop a school-choice plan for Ohio.[16] Brennan and other prominent Republicans argued that the choice system envisioned by the commission would eventually save tax dollars by creating a public-private system that involved more parents and students.[17]

At the outset, this effort attracted bipartisan interest as the general assembly considered creation of a "pilot" voucher program for Cleveland and other cities. That pilot would have granted vouchers for up to seven thousand students as part of a five-year study to see whether private schools do a better job than public schools.[18] It would have included randomized trials to gauge the academic impact of vouchers on poor children in big cities. "What we're trying to do here is a test. Let's get some answers," said Willowick Democrat Daniel P. Troy.[19] But Democrats ultimately revolted against the plan because the money for vouchers would come out of state funding for school districts—and the teacher unions hated the idea.[20]

Ohio's early exploration of vouchers permanently severed any link between school choice and bipartisanship in the Buckeye State, which later made charter schools more partisan here than in many places. Even as these quasi-independent public schools were launched under bipartisan auspices in Indiana, Massachusetts, Minnesota, Colorado, California, the District of Columbia, and elsewhere, all forms of school choice in Ohio had, by 1995, become exclusively a GOP thing. Choice opponents, such as State School Board president Oliver Ocasek, saw the governor's commission on choice as nothing but an attempt by conservatives to bury district public schools. "This [voucher] plan is the greatest threat to the public schools we have ever faced," Ocasek declared.[21]

While Voinovich's and Brennan's initial plan for a statewide voucher program could not overcome such opposition, in 1995 a voucher program was finally created for Cleveland. According to Brennan, "To reach this point had taken the recommendations of the Governor's Task Force and a legislative process in which the recommendations of the Ohio Scholarship Plan were killed and reborn and killed again."[22] The constitutionality of the Cleveland program would be debated and litigated until it was upheld by the United States Supreme Court in 2002, a decision that reverberated across the land—and also foreshadowed the successful effort, in 2006, to expand voucher eligibility across Ohio.

The Charter School Concept

Into this already stormy political environment came charter schools as a serious policy idea. Called "community schools" in Ohio,[23] they operate independently of traditional districts. Each enters into a performance contract with a sponsoring organization (also known as an "authorizer") acting as general overseer. If the school fails to live up to its contract, its sponsor can revoke the charter or choose not to renew it. In return for results-based accountability, charter schools are supposed to be freed from many of the regulations governing district schools and thereby enabled to map their own path to innovation and, it was hoped, educational quality.

Charter schools are schools of choice, attended by children whose families opt to enroll in them and staffed by educators who choose to teach there. According to Harvard political scientist Paul Peterson, "The common characteristics of charter schools are twofold. First, the entity operating the school is ordinarily not a government agency, though it may receive most of its operating revenue from either the state or a local school board. Second, charter schools do not serve students within a specific attendance boundary; instead they recruit students from a large catchment area that may be beyond the attendance boundaries of traditional public schools. As a result, they must persuade parents that their offerings are superior to those provided by traditional public schools in their vicinity."[24] Petro's Cleveland audit underscored the need for such education innovations and alternatives. (When it came out in 1996, the city's voucher program was already serving more than three thousand children in just its first year of operation.) The state auditor described himself as a big supporter of public education but argued that, in too many district schools, it was simply failing too many children. More of the same was unacceptable and experiments involving fresh approaches to teaching and learning were vital. He and other school choice supporters simply replied to critics, "You won't know until you try it."[25] Petro added that "establishing charter school laws will not solve all of the problems for all of the students, but it may solve some of the problems for some of the students."[26]

Ohio's first significant charter bill was introduced by Sally Perz, a Toledo Republican, a few days after Petro's Cleveland audit was released. Its champions were all fellow Republicans. In the House, both Perz, a former junior high school math teacher, and Michael A. Fox, also a former teacher, fought tirelessly for charters. Their ally in the senate was Cooper Snyder, a Republican from southwestern Ohio, who chaired that chamber's Education and Retirement Committee.

The test data were irrefutable. Children trapped in dismal district schools urgently needed something better. Promises that things were slowly improving rang hollow to parents with daughters and sons in broken schools that manifestly were not getting better. Their kids couldn't wait another decade for a fix. At the start, charters were seen as escape hatches for such children. Proponents also promised that they would serve as centers of innovation, research, and development that would in time benefit children across public education. They would generate competition that would spur districts toward sustained academic reform. They would cost less than district schools. And they would produce superior academic results. Fox said as much in 1999 when he commented that "the expectations I have for charter schools are higher than the expectations I have for public schools because charter schools have a flexibility public schools don't have."[27]

This quintuple promise—salubrious competition, stronger academic outcomes, inventive approaches, parsimony, and immediate relief for the educationally oppressed—may have been a tad naïve but charter advocates were making it across America. And they were succeeding.

In 1996, nineteen states had enacted charter legislation and some 250 charter schools were serving about 20,000 pupils. Just two years later, thirty-four states and the District of Columbia had charter laws and some 1,200 schools were educating more than a quarter million students. By 1999, the number of schools had risen to almost 1,700.[28] Charters were also one of the fastest growing business sectors in America at the time and—outside Ohio—they enjoyed bipartisan support. In May 2000, President Bill Clinton called for establishing 3,000 of them by 2002, and requested $175 million in fiscal 2001 to help jump-start a new round of such schools.[29] (In recent months, President Obama has been even more ardent in his support of this kind of education reform.)

For a time, bipartisanship even extended to the teacher unions. Albert Shanker, the president of the American Federation of Teachers (AFT), released a report at the AFT's August 1996 national conference in Cincinnati that endorsed charter schools. Shanker, who had been the first major figure in American education to propose charter schools publicly (at the National Press Club in 1988), told his delegates that the "goal of charter schools should not be innovation for its own sake, but innovation for improved student achievement."[30]

Following his lead, Ohio teacher unions also expressed mild support for charter schools. Michael N. Billirakis, president of the Ohio Education Association, told a reporter that his organization had always supported the concept.[31] Said Ron Marec, president of the Ohio Federation of Teachers, "In a lot of ways, what would be in a good charter-school bill are in Perz's bill."[32] But it was also clear from the start that the unions' view of charter schools was radically different from that of GOP lawmakers. The teacher groups were OK with district-sponsored charters but wanted nothing to do with truly independent charter operators, especially those free from collective bargaining contracts. In Shanker's vision, small groups of teachers and parents would submit research-based proposals to educate relatively small numbers of kids in novel ways. A panel composed of local school board and teacher union officials would review each such proposal. Once granted a charter, the school would be left alone for five to ten years.[33] Under this arrangement, schools would be free from certain contractual provisions such as those governing length of school day and year, but their teachers would still be unionized. It was also clear that, under the unions' conception of charter schools, these schools could operate only with the assent of both union and district. The education establishment would still be firmly in control.

An exasperated Sally Perz exclaimed during the protracted debate around her bill that "every one of the school establishment groups are for charter schools if their little list is included. . . . They want charter schools if they are fully funded by the state. They want charter schools if there is collective bargaining. These things add up to business as usual, and you can't have it both ways. The aim is to be unique, and each school should be free of as much regulation as possible so they can be as innovative as possible."[34] Perz concluded, "If we wrote a bill giving everybody what they wanted, we'd never have a charter school in Ohio."[35]

Her bill passed the house, where rural and suburban legislators favored it because their constituents were being taxed to fund broken schools in districts incapable of or unwilling to fix themselves. But it ultimately perished in the senate at the hands of the teacher unions, the Ohio School Boards Association, and the Buckeye Association of School Administrators. These groups feared charters would drain money and students away from district schools, steal control from local officials, threaten union teaching positions, and gradually threaten public education itself. In the end, even their lip service to the idea of charters-as-innovators faded away. "Charter schools represent a raid on the public treasury to fund private schools,"[36] claimed minority leader Ben Espy, D-Columbus, and a close ally of the teacher unions.

Thomas Richey, superintendent of the Winton Woods City Schools, illustrated Perz's point. "I'm not opposed to charter schools," he explained. "What I'm opposed to is, number one, they're not going to be required to follow the same requirements, and, number two, they're going to take district funds."[37] Such claims triggered fierce rebuttals from GOP lawmakers like Cooper Snyder. "It's not the district's money," he said. "It's the money that we as a community have to put out to spend on kids to educate them," he argued. "The public schools, as now operated, are failing to do that."[38] But to no avail—for the moment.

The Arrival of Charters

The idea of charter schools resurfaced in Governor Voinovich's 1997 biennial budget (House Bill 215). He regarded them as drivers of urban school reform. "If there's any area we're going to be focusing on, it's urban schools,"[39] Voinovich said in an interview at the end of 1996. With the GOP in control of the legislature, it was obvious that the budget would reflect Republican school funding views, would address district-level accountability, and would have a place for charter schools. Voinovich proposed a two-year, $36.14 billion state budget that earmarked $8.5 billion for public education, especially for improving urban districts.

A summary of his proposal noted that absenteeism, dropout rates, suspensions, and expulsions were all higher in Ohio's urban districts than in the rest of the state and that their student performance was below the state average.[40] His plan was carefully calculated: urban districts would get more money but would also face greater scrutiny and accountability, and their monopoly on public education would now face competition from charter schools. Like education reformers in other states who sweetened the bitter pill of change by coating it with the honey of additional dollars, he provided a whopping 12 percent boost in state spending on education over the previous biennium, including the following:

- $87 million for all-day kindergarten in the Big 8 districts
- $15 million for twenty-one urban districts to deal with discipline problems
- $6 million for Urban Leadership Academies providing professional development for principals and teachers
- $1.8 million for high school dropouts to complete requirements for a diploma
- $100 million for renovations and repairs of urban school buildings with local districts required to match state funds and another $200 million was sought for the sixty-one poorest districts

The accountability side of the proposal included $1 million for a performance review of all the urban districts akin to Petro's Cleveland audit. Voinovich also proposed a $4.5 million charter school pilot project in Lucas County (Toledo). Gregory Browning, director of the state Office of Management and Budget, explained that "there is a sense that the governance structure is very rigid in schools, and it is hoped that charter schools will promote reform and entrepreneurialism and a sense of ownership and everything that goes along with that." Legislator Mike Fox added that "lawmakers must continue doing all they can to help public schools but also must provide 'a bypass to the existing system' with vouchers and charter schools which eliminate bureaucracy and promote innovation."[41]

Despite Cleveland's educational infamy, Toledo was chosen for the pilot charter program because no Cleveland lawmakers wanted the program in their backyard while Perz had revved up excitement in Toledo. Indeed, she had already recruited many potential charter partners, including the University of Toledo.

As the budget bill worked its way through the senate and then the house-senate conference committee in the summer of 1997, the DeRolph decision was front and center in lawmakers' minds. The supreme court had ruled in March that Ohio's school funding system was unconstitutional. Writing for the majority, Justice Francis E. Sweeney said, "we send a clear message to lawmakers; the time has come to fix the system. Let there be no misunderstanding. Ohio's public school financing scheme must undergo complete, systemic overhaul."[42]

The court gave state leaders a single year to prepare a remedy. Given the bluntness of its language, legislators realized that more money would indeed be needed. House Finance Committee chair Tom Johnson noted that "we've fine-tuned the overall budget to allow for even greater levels of education spending. In light of the recent Supreme Court decision on school funding, the conference committee built on the Senate's efforts to provide stronger state support of primary and secondary schools."[43] Senate Finance Chairman Roy L. Ray added that "we've taken care of education big time. The money we've put into K–12 is unprecedented."[44]

In signing the budget measure on July 1, 1997, Voinovich sought to make clear to the supreme court as well as the wider public that school funding was the state's top priority. "I am proud of this budget, of which nearly a third is allocated for Ohio's schools,"[45] he said, pointing to a 13 percent increase in state aid over the biennium. Besides allocating substantial new sums for urban schools, the measure contained the rudiments of a new charter school program:

- It established a "pilot" community school program in Toledo (allowing charters to be established in any school district having a majority of its territory in Lucas County).
- It allowed (in Lucas County) both start-up schools—charters started from scratch—and schools converted from existing district schools.
- It allowed any district in the state to convert existing public schools to charters.

Thus, Ohio's charter school program was conceived as part of the state's first budgetary response to the supreme court's ruling that the old school funding system was unconstitutional. Yet this wasn't the end of either the funding contretemps or the charter school debate, for the DeRolph plaintiffs insisted that even this generous biennial spending plan failed to meet the court's requirements and they prepared to haul the state back into court.

Republicans didn't want this and sought to forestall further litigation by spending still more on schools. Indeed, even as Voinovich and conservative lawmakers groused about the court, they began to push for additional taxes to funnel further dollars to the state's poorer schools. Just days after the budget was signed into law, Voinovich sent lawmakers a $1.2 billion-a-year supplemental funding proposal, including a one percent increase in the sales tax and a 12-cents-a-pack tax on cigarettes. This was in direct response to the court's ruling and sought to meet its demand for a redesigned school funding system.

If the court was going to insist on a new way of paying for public education, Republicans wanted to ensure that the extra billions were accompanied by enforceable performance standards for students and financial accountability for districts. According to Tom Needles, Voinovich's executive assistant at the time, "The goal with the school-funding plan—it's a whole-cloth approach—is that funding and accountability must go hand in hand."[46]

Not everyone welcomed this combination. Some conservatives in the house criticized Voinovich's supplemental spending plan because of its tax increases. And both house and senate Democrats objected that it didn't direct as much money to urban and rural schools as they thought the court had demanded. Lawmakers argued well into the autumn. In the midst of it, the *Columbus Dispatch* noted, "when the swirl of competing ideas becomes so thick, so contradictory and—most unfortunately—so laden with partisan and ideological doodads, legislators should remember the most important political principle of all—the willingness to compromise."[47] In an angry letter to the senate Democratic leader, senate president Richard Finan admonished, "If you and your colleagues have specific ideas on the best approach to addressing the school funding issues, now is the time for them to surface. Although that may not serve you politically, it will serve the interest of those who have placed their trust in us to oversee state government in Ohio."[48]

Among other changes, lawmakers broke the accountability plan into two separate measures. Taken together, Senate Bill 55 and House Bill 412, both introduced in July 1997 and enacted in August, included new proficiency testing; more rigorous high school graduation requirements; reading readiness for fourth-graders; and audits for financially troubled districts. No charter school language appeared in either bill as introduced.

But at the last minute, and without any apparent public debate, a provision was inserted into Senate Bill 55 to permit the launch of start-up charter schools in any Big 8 district.

That language appeared in the bill after Mike Fox made clear that he would support a sales tax increase, anathema to most house Republicans, only if the governor and legislative leaders agreed to a much-expanded charter program.[49] Because of Fox's quid pro quo, charters advanced in Ohio far more rapidly than anyone had expected. The Lucas County pilot had been approved only weeks earlier but Senate Bill 55 expanded it eight-fold. The amended measure, which passed with no Democratic support in the house, made the State Board of Education into a charter school sponsor. The upshot was that Ohio became a major charter player as a sort of by-product of the most contentious school funding debate in state history.

Notes

1. The number for private institutions comes from Todd Jones, President and General Counsel of the Association of Independent Colleges and Universities of Ohio, March 30, 2010.
2. Herb Asher, interview by Mike Lafferty, July 22, 2008.
3. Joe Hallett, "DeRolph Seen as Worthy Milestone, but Continued Fix Is Questioned," *Columbus Dispatch*, January 21, 2007, 5B.
4. Bricker & Eckler, LLP. *Chronology of the DeRolph School Funding Litigation: Dale R. DeRolph et al. v. The State of Ohio et al.*, http://www.bricker.com/legalservices/practice/Education/SchoolFund/chronology.asp.
5. Ibid.
6. Joe Hallett, "What Went On in the Supreme Court," *Columbus Dispatch*, March 18, 2007, http://www.dispatch.com/live/contentbe/dispatch/2007/03/18/20070318-A1-00.html.
7. The court decided to end the case, at least in part, because Ohio had made real progress toward equity in the late 1990s and 2000s. For example, in 2000 *Education Week* gave Ohio a D+ for school funding equity; in 2008, Ohio had risen into the top half of states with a grade of B–. In its 2008 *Funding Gap* report, the Education Trust cited Ohio as one of just ten states that had successfully decreased the gaps between low- and high-poverty districts.
8. Editorial, "Judicial Lawmaking High Court Wreaks Havoc on Ohio Schools," *Columbus Dispatch*, March 25, 1997, 14A.
9. Mary Beth Lane, "School Officials Call Audit Accurate; Teachers Question District's Solutions," *Cleveland Plain Dealer*, June 16, 1996, 1B.
10. James Bradshaw, "Audit Parallels School Woes Here with Cleveland's," *Columbus Dispatch*, March 16, 1996, 1E.

11. Benjamin Marrison and Thomas Suddes, "Schools Doomed without Drastic Cuts, Audit Says Plan Would Slash $73 Million from Cleveland Budget," *Cleveland Plain Dealer*, March 15, 1996, 1A.

12. Bradshaw, "Audit Parallels School Woes."

13. Mary Beth Lane, "Legislator Proposes Charter Schools," *Cleveland Plain Dealer*, March 15, 1997, 1A.

14. Ibid.

15. Lee Leonard, "Suburban, Rural Districts Shouldn't Be Penalized, Lawmakers Say," *Columbus Dispatch*, January 16, 1997, 6C.

16. David L. Brennan, *Victory for Kids: The Cleveland School Voucher Case* (Beverly Hills, CA: New Millennium Press, 2002), 33.

17. Jonathan Riskind, "Panel against Using Taxes for School Vouchers," *Columbus Dispatch*, October 6, 1993, 6B.

18. Mary Yost, "Legislative Plan Seeks Test of Public vs. Private Schools," *Columbus Dispatch*, January 24, 1992, 4D.

19. Ibid.

20. The Cleveland vouchers were indeed deducted from the Cleveland school system's share of state dollars for poor children known as "Disadvantaged Pupil Impact Aid," but, as Brennan predicted, the program did save taxpayers money. According to a study by the Government Accounting Office in 2001, "The per pupil amount expended for the voucher program in Cleveland for the 1999–2000 school year was $1,832," which was a far smaller amount than "the total per-pupil state aid ($4,910) that was provided to the Cleveland public school district" (U.S. General Accounting Office, Report to the Honorable Judd Gregg, United States Senate, "School Vouchers: Publicly Funded Programs in Cleveland and Milwaukee," August 2001).

21. Riskind, "Panel against Using Taxes."

22. Brennan, *Victory for Kids*, 36.

23. This nomenclature is intended to avoid confusion with private schools that operate under "charters" issued by the State Board of Education.

24. Paul E. Peterson, "Choice in American Education," in *A Primer on America's Schools*, ed. Terry M. Moe, 258–59 (Stanford, CA: Hoover Institution Press, 2001).

25. Lee Leonard, "School Districts Must Make Sure Numbers Add Up, Petro Says," *Columbus Dispatch*, April 24, 1997, 8D.

26. Jim Petro, "Cleveland City School District Performance Audit," *Ohio Auditor of State*, March 15, 1996, 4–26.

27. Scott Stephens, "Lessons Learned at Charter School Debate over Effectiveness Continues, as State OKs 37 More 'Community Schools,'" *Cleveland Plain Dealer*, August 1, 1999, 1B.

28. Peterson, "Choice in American Education," 258.

29. Archived White House Press Release, "President Clinton Announces $16 Million in Support for Charter Schools," May 4, 2000, http://www.ed.gov/PressReleases/05-2000/0504.html.

30. Catherine Candisky, "Union's Push May Not Budge Charter School Bill," *Columbus Dispatch*, August 4, 1996, 3C.

31. Catherine Candisky, "Senate to Consider School Bill; Measure to Allow Charter Schools in Ohio Amended," *Columbus Dispatch*, March 24, 1996, 1D.

32. Candisky, "Union's Push."

33. Richard D. Kahlenberg, "Commentary: The Charter School Idea Turns 20," *Education Week*, March 25, 2008.

34. Candisky, "Union's Push."

35. Ibid.

36. Catherine Candisky, "Charter School Proposal Can't Get Enough Support," *Columbus Dispatch*, March 28, 1996, 2B.

37. Associated Press, "Some Hope to Start Own School," *Columbus Dispatch*, March 18, 1996, 3C.

38. Ibid.

39. Lee Leonard, "Budget, School Funding to Occupy Lawmakers in 1997," *Columbus Dispatch*, January 1, 1997, 1C.

40. Catherine Candisky, "Big Money Aimed at Big-City Schools," *Columbus Dispatch*, February 4, 1997, 1A.

41. Catherine Candisky, "Schools Need More Than Money, Forum Told," *Columbus Dispatch*, June 11, 1997, 3B.

42. Duane St. Clair, "4–3 Ruling Ends Fight Begun in '91," *Columbus Dispatch*, March 25, 1997, 1A.

43. Catherine Candisky, "Schools Get $13.3 Billion," *Columbus Dispatch*, June 24, 1997, 1C.

44. Ibid.

45. Lee Leonard, "$36.1 Billion State Budget Gets Governor's Signature," *Columbus Dispatch*, July 1, 1997, 1B.

46. "Legislators Gear Up for Education Reforms," *Columbus Dispatch*, July 13, 1997, 1E.

47. Editorial, "Duty of Debacle Lawmakers Risk Court-Imposed Solution," *Columbus Dispatch*, July 27, 1997, 2E.

48. Catherine Candisky and Lee Leonard, "Lawmakers Accuse Each Other of Playing Politics over School Funding," *Columbus Dispatch*, July 18, 1997, 2C.

49. Senator Jeff Jacobson, interview by Mike Lafferty, June 12, 2008.

3

Urban School Reform

Part I

When Ohio issued its first district and school-level report cards in 1998, they confirmed what most Daytonians had known for at least a decade: the Gem City's public schools were in academic tatters. By the state's reckoning, Dayton and Cleveland were the two worst districts in Ohio. At the time, the Dayton public schools (DPS) served about 26,000 students, employed 3,847 people (half of them teachers), and had an operating budget of $203 million. But its academic performance was woeful. As summed up by the *Cleveland Plain Dealer*'s education reporter, "With dwindling enrollments and abysmal test scores, the [Dayton] school district looked like a poster child for all that was wrong with the big urban school systems. Too many students were dropping out. Too many never came at all. There was little or no discipline. Teacher morale sagged. School board members bickered. Deficits soared."[1]

As in every troubled American city, district schools were the only education option for families lacking the means to pay for private or parochial schools or escape to the suburbs. Dayton's neediest children suffered most. The district's 1998 achievement data in every subject showed far fewer African American than white fourth-graders meeting state levels of minimum proficiency. On the reading test, 71 percent of white students achieved proficiency, while 59 percent of black youngsters did. In math, 45 percent of white students hit the target compared with 28 percent of black pupils.[2]

By now, business leaders, many parents, and even the district superintendent craved major changes. Up to that point, nothing had worked, whether a reform plan from a new superintendent, a changed school board policy, or a fresh infusion of tax-levy dollars. Discouragement, even desperation, was setting in, especially when state report cards affixed hard numbers to what most people already sensed. Civic leaders, hearkening back to the tradition of community oversight from John Patterson's day but also needing decently educated workers for their own firms, were especially frustrated.

Ron Budzik, then an executive with the Mead Corporation—which was long based in Dayton before joining the corporate exodus from the city— had worked long hours on school issues. Yet his efforts had yielded only mounting frustration at the failure of the city's education and business establishments to effect any improvement. Budzik had helped, for example, to found the Alliance for Education, dedicated to advancing professional development among Dayton-area teachers and improving the capacity of local school districts to succeed. "That program worked for quite a few years," Budzik recalled in 2008, "but in terms of inner-city schools, there was little you could look out at and say it was successful. It was pretty obvious that the district had poor proficiency results, mixed academic success and some truly poor performing buildings."[3]

As DPS was bumping along a rocky bottom, the Thomas B. Fordham Foundation emerged as a new player on the local scene. When Thelma Fordham Pruett died with no heirs and left the remains of her first husband's fortune to the foundation, its small board found itself with an endowment of some $35 million and an obligation under the tax code to spend at least 5 percent of that sum every year on charitable activity. This was far more than the foundation had ever dealt with before and obviously called for a more professional operation than the annual lunch at which trustees were accustomed to allocating modest sums to worthy local charities.

The trustees asked one of their own members, Chester E. Finn, Jr., if he would consider leading a revamped foundation. Although a Dayton native, Finn had long lived in Washington and his own career was devoted to primary-secondary education. He had worked in various government, academic, and private sector roles and was known as a prolific, take-no-prisoners education critic. In the mid-1990s, his primary job was senior fellow in the Washington office of the Hudson Institute think tank, where he engaged in research on charter schools, among other education issues, and co-led, with the historian Diane Ravitch, an informal league of school reformers called the Educational Excellence Network.

Finn and the other Fordham trustees reached a meeting of the minds: he would assume responsibility for leading the foundation and directing its day-to-day work if it were headquartered in Washington; if it focused its resources and energies on the reform of primary-secondary education, both nationally and in Dayton; if it embraced the principles of the Educational Excellence Network; and if its board expanded to include others (including Ravitch) who shared those principles and had both knowledge and ardor for education reform.

The reborn foundation's enhanced board of education experts, civic and business leaders, including several from the Dayton area, would gradually turn Fordham into a national educational force. But beginning in 1997, it was also active and visible on the Dayton scene, where its staff and trustees strove to put some of its ideas to work in the real world of urban education, particularly in the creation of better options for needy families with children stuck in failing schools.

Initially, the foundation sought to work with DPS but soon realized that the school system didn't want, or couldn't bring itself to accept, the help and was allergic to major changes—essentially the same problem that local business leaders had long faced in dealing with DPS. District officials wanted money but not guidance or hands-on involvement. Finn told the *Cleveland Plain Dealer* in 2001 that "we would love to help reform the school system, but it has shown very little inclination to want help of that kind."[4]

The PACE of Change

Fordham board members and staff saw too many Dayton parents forced to send their kids to inadequate, even dreadful schools and understood that they needed better alternatives. Making an end run around the uncooperative district, Fordham and several Dayton civic leaders and philanthropists forged a partnership to provide families with choices. In 1997, it appeared that the quickest way to do this—while perhaps also spurring the district to improve—was to develop a privately funded scholarship program, which was dubbed Parents Advancing Choice in Education (PACE). The idea was to provide financial assistance—privately funded vouchers, really—to low-income Dayton parents so they could afford to move their daughters and sons into better suburban public schools or private schools.

By the 1990s, school-choice programs and policies were turning up all across the United States. Children from the District of Columbia whose families could afford to pay tuition had been attending class in Maryland or Virginia public schools for years. Magnet schools were ubiquitous in most urban systems and some states permitted students to attend schools in adjoining districts. Minnesota allowed its children to attend any public school in the state and several other jurisdictions had copied this open-enrollment model. But except for a handful of selective schools (like Cincinnati's esteemed Walnut Hills High School), public school choice had never caught on in Ohio. Certainly there was no evidence that suburban districts would welcome children from poor inner-city precincts.

Youngsters in some of America's most educationally troubled cities gradually began to receive additional choices with the emergence of private scholarship programs in the 1990s. Although only Milwaukee (and, more recently, Cleveland) had publicly funded voucher programs for needy children at this time, the privately financed kind was spreading. As reconstructed by the U.S. General Accounting Office, this movement got its "start in 1991 when an Indianapolis businessman founded a local program that provided tuition assistance to about 750 low-income students in grade kindergarten through 8. . . . By 1997, there were 31 local programs offering over 12,000 privately funded vouchers to K–12 students in 18 states plus the District of Columbia."[5]

Such programs assisted low-income children to leave their public schools for private schools of their parents' choosing. In New York City, for example, investment banker Peter M. Flanigan championed the idea of such grants to enable students in failing public schools to attend private—mostly Catholic parochial—schools in Gotham. In fact, Flanigan, whom Finn knew from the days when they both worked in the Nixon White House, helped to plant the PACE idea with Fordham.

Fordham's board liked the idea. In February 1997, board member Bruno V. Manno (a former Ohioan, indeed an alumnus of the University of Dayton, now a nationally recognized education expert based in Washington) made the case for it in a memo entitled "Proposed Fordham Scholars Program—Private Scholarships for Low-Income Dayton Families." Manno said such a program could achieve three important goals.

First, it could widen educational opportunities for needy children—which was the primary goal of nearly all choice programs. Second, it could serve as a national model for school choice and trigger an important political debate in Dayton and beyond. Third, a scholarship program such as this could inject competition into the public education system, thereby raising the level of teaching and learning in all schools. Manno hoped that "it could have a catalytic effect on the schools of Dayton." But he also acknowledged that there was vigorous debate "with adamant opposition from the teacher unions and the rest of the education establishment and strong support from conservatives, progressive Democrats, minorities, and business leaders."

At its launch in 1998, PACE represented a significant partnership between Fordham and Dayton business/community leaders—and a major commitment of Fordham's own resources. The idea of using private scholarships as vehicles for children in troubled schools to attend a private school or a better public school in nearby districts excited other leading Daytonians, including businessmen Matt Diggs and Mervyn Alphonso, attorney (and Fordham board member) Tom Holton, and Reverend Daryl

Ward, a prominent black Baptist pastor, all of whom saw this as a direct benefit to needy children and a way to prod the public schools to action, whether they liked it or not. Early PACE boosters also included local entrepreneur/philanthropist Clay Mathile (then owner of Iams Pet Foods) and other successful Catholic businessmen such as Richard Glennon.

They were concerned about public education in Dayton as well as declining parochial school enrollments caused by Catholics joining the flight from urban neighborhoods where many such schools were still located. PACE offered a chance for inner-city kids to receive a better education and also a chance for parochial schools to fill empty seats.

Putting PACE together was a major undertaking. Over a four-month period in 1997, Fordham staff and trustees strove to assemble a board of prominent business and university leaders, philanthropists, investors, and a physician. Scholarship money had to be raised, and Fordham insisted that a research component be incorporated. Additionally, partner schools that would accept PACE scholarships needed to be brought on board, and children recruited into the program. It was decided that only low-income students would qualify for assistance and that a lottery would determine which youngsters got scholarships. Parents would have to scrape up half the money for their children's tuition, with individual scholarships capped at $1,200 per year. (Catholic schools in Dayton were then charging about $2,400 for tuition.) The PACE trustees wanted to help—but they also wanted parents to be invested.

The demand appeared to be there. Fordham commissioned a 1998 survey of Daytonians to probe their attitudes toward education reform. One question read: "Suppose you could send your oldest child to any public, private, or church-related school of your choice, with tuition paid for by the government. Would you send your oldest child to the school he or she now attends, or to a different school?" Only 37 percent of Dayton parents said they would keep their child in his or her current school while 59 percent would opt for a different school.[6] In other words, well over half of Dayton parents were ready to forsake DPS if given the chance.

But the PACE idea fell flat with suburban public schools. Their officials didn't have to accept the city kids and made clear that they wouldn't— much as suburban Cleveland schools refused to accept public-voucher students (and still do). Even reform-minded superintendents like Kettering's Stephen Scovic—who in the late 1990s was a serious supporter and advocate for bringing high-quality charter schools to Dayton—rejected PACE's request for access to his district schools. "I feel it's a process to undermine urban education rather than solve urban education's problems,"[7] Scovic told *The Dayton Daily News*. (Privately, he indicated to Fordham staff that in his long public school career he had found white suburbanites in southern Ohio—presumably including the residents of Kettering—exceptionally inhospitable to any form of racial integration.) Absent willing participation by suburban public school districts, PACE became exclusively a program to assist parents to send their children to local private and parochial schools.

Despite obvious yearning by Dayton parents for something different, PACE was launched in the autumn of 1998 with just 515 scholarship holders, although funding was available for nearly twice that number. The shortfall was likely due in part to critics who noisily branded it an attack on the public schools. Still, these first PACE scholarships were enough to create a serious buzz in the community and set off alarm bells at DPS headquarters. Fewer pupils meant less state aid, and district leaders feared that PACE would drain off children and the state and federal dollars that accompanied them. Superintendent James Williams called PACE a "wake-up call" and warned that the "district would have to cut staff if it lost the $3.6 million in state funding that would be eliminated by the loss of 1,000 Dayton students to private schools."[8]

As it turned out, Williams's concerns were overblown, at least at the outset. Almost half of the first crop of scholarship recipients were poor children already attending private schools. PACE provided financial aid so their families could afford to keep them there. Remaining scholarship winners came from a cross-section of area school districts, not just Dayton. As PACE board member Mervyn Alphonso predicted, "the student-loss impact will be spread around because poor students live all over the county."[9]

PACE also encountered plenty of naysayers. Because of Fordham's strong support and high profile, many Daytonians supposed that the initiative was exclusively a foundation endeavor. Some even termed the scholarships "Fordham vouchers." This made it easier to attack the program as an experiment being foisted upon the community by a Washington-based "conservative critic of public education."[10]

In time, it became clear that while Fordham may have been the catalyst, PACE enjoyed broad local support, including funds from the Mathile Family Foundation and the Louise Kramer Foundation. It was also led by Dayton-based talent, initially by T. J. Wallace, a former Dayton (Catholic) high school principal. Its board consisted entirely of prominent Daytonians. And in time, it developed a substantial parent outreach program managed by a community activist and spark plug named Daria Dillard Stone. In 2008, Stone reflected on PACE and its impact: "The public school system was not the best it could be. They needed competition. We were never after public schools, but we did make them better in the long run."[11]

She was not alone in this conclusion. *Dayton Daily News* education reporter Scott Elliott, reflecting upon PACE's first decade, put it this way:

> When it launched in 1998, privately funded PACE was a rare example of a program designed to help parents overcome the cost obstacles to giving their kids the type of education the family desired. Pre-dating charter schools, PACE was also Dayton's first foray into a school choice program.
>
> A decade later, PACE has helped 6,000 kids attend private schools with about $9 million in scholarships. And the city's now vast array of school choice options include more than 30 charter schools along with both publicly-funded vouchers and the PACE scholarships available for parents who want private schools.
>
> The new options have completely re-made Dayton into a nationally recognized school-choice mecca. And PACE was an early catalyst for change.[12]

Recruitment of children was somewhat complicated by PACE's research element, which wouldn't have been there but for Fordham's insistence that the scholarship program be data driven and open to rigorous evaluation. The foundation had many contacts in the social science community, people who realized that the growing choice movement had put Dayton on the education research map. Fordham persuaded Harvard's Paul Peterson and a team of analysts to evaluate the scholarship program along with similar programs in New York City and Washington, DC. (Fordham also found the money to underwrite Dayton's inclusion in that study.)

The basic question was whether or not students exercising school choice with the help of these scholarships outperformed their peers who remained in traditional public schools. The research team agreed to include PACE in its evaluation if they could conduct a randomized field trial in Dayton. This was a state-of-the-art method that Peterson analogized to medical research: "In medical research, the randomized field trial is required before a pill can be marketed, because a lottery is used to decide whether a patient gets the pill—or, in this case, whether a family gets a voucher or not. When you compare the lottery winners with those who did not win, you compare two groups that were essentially the same when the field trial began. Any differences that appear later must be due to the pill, or, in this case, the voucher."[13] Peterson wanted at least 1,300 children from Dayton for this analysis, half receiving scholarships and half for the control group. The first-year enrollment of PACE scholarship students fell short, so the research design was modified to accommodate a smaller number of scholarship students and a smaller control group. But proceed it did. And in February 2000,

Peterson and William G. Howell released their first report, "School Choice in Dayton, Ohio: An Evaluation after One Year," which found the following:

- African American students attending private school scored seven percentage points higher on the Iowa Test of Basic Skills (ITBS) in math and five points higher in reading than did the African American students in the public school control group.
- Non-African American students in private schools did not score significantly different than their public school counterparts in either mathematics or reading.

That such scholarships had a positive impact on the academic achievement of black youngsters but not on other pupil groups was also the key conclusion reached in Peterson's larger study, released in August 2000. In all three communities, he found, the average two-year gain for African Americans was 6.3 percent, virtually identical to the outcome in Dayton. On the other hand, in all three cities the scholarship programs had no significant impact on the achievement of nonblack students. The analysts were stumped. "At this time," they admitted, "the evaluation team is unable to explain why school vouchers have positive effects on African-American students but no detectable effects on others."[14]

PACE received a shot in the arm in 1999 when, with Fordham's encouragement, the New York–based Children's Scholarship Fund (CSF) selected Dayton as one of thirty-six cities in which to invest sizable sums in the form of matching dollars to support private scholarships for needy children. CSF was a national program funded by venture capitalist Teddy Forstmann and Wal-Mart heir John Walton. By 1999, it was providing school vouchers to about 40,000 pupils in some forty cities. Its Dayton commitment came to $375,000 per annum.

These outside resources, along with a better marketing effort, helped PACE to grow quickly from a $615,000 program in 1998 to $1.18 million the following year, when 853 children received scholarships. Over the nine years from 1998 through 2007, as journalist Scott Elliott reported, PACE provided more than 6,000 scholarships valued at about $8.6 million. Fordham invested about $2.5 million in this program—by far its largest financial commitment during this period.

The System's Reaction

DPS superintendent James Williams didn't just sit by and watch his students line up for the scholarship lottery in order to flee his schools. He sought to be proactive and, when Ohio's charter law was passed in the summer of 1997, he seized upon it and proposed to convert five troubled DPS schools into charters. He outlined that plan in a white paper entitled "Re-Creating the Learning Community: A Proposal to Reconstitute Five Schools." Williams wanted to turn three of the district's lowest-performing elementary schools and two of its worst middle schools into "conversion" charter schools. His plan contained forceful language and at least one radical concept for union-friendly Dayton.

He intimated that poor pupil achievement was at least partly linked to poor teachers and noted that "the goal of reconstitution is to improve student academic achievement *and the removal of a dysfunctional community of educators who for all intents and purposes have given up on the youngsters they serve* [emphasis added]." Williams continued, "Improving student academic achievement can be accomplished by changing the instructional delivery system in a dramatic way—a plan that requires the re-staffing of a school, revising how the 'new' staff provides instruction and changing other elements of conventional schooling such as calendar, technology, schedule, and resource allocation."[15]

The five schools he targeted, out of forty-nine in the district, enrolled about 10 percent of DPS pupils. His plan called for a "reconstitution committee" to oversee the effort and provide technical and political support. It would comprise representatives from the district, the University of Dayton, the business community, and—remarkably—the Fordham Foundation. The proposed governing authority for the reconstituted schools would be a who's who of Dayton civic, education, and business leaders. Principals and teachers in the affected schools would have to reapply for their jobs.

Additionally, the schools would enjoy contract waivers from the teachers' union to facilitate innovation in the length of their days and years, as well as the opportunity to pay their instructors more. The most controversial part of the plan called for outsourcing day-to-day operations of the schools to the for-profit school-management company known as the Edison Project. At that time, Edison, based in New York City, was operating twenty-five public schools with thirteen thousand students in eight other states.

Williams was ahead of his time, at least in Ohio. When he formally introduced the plan in January 1998, he argued that DPS needed to be out front on the charter school issue. The city needed to turn this new opportunity to its advantage. "I strongly believe that if we don't change, someone else is going to change it for us," he said.[16] Williams explained to his board that charter supporters could bypass DPS completely and open start-up schools under the sponsorship of the Ohio Department of Education.

In seeking board approval, Williams made clear that, under the charter law, teachers in the conversion schools would be unionized but that school-management teams would make the final decisions on which teachers they wanted. Williams went on to assure the union that teachers not reemployed by the reconstituted schools would still have jobs in other DPS schools. He also reiterated time and again for the union and his board that start-up charter schools do not have unionized teachers and—should these emerge in Dayton—they would operate free of any relationship with either union or school board.

As proposed, the reconstitution plan enjoyed the support of a significant cross-section of the community, including the presidents of the University of Dayton, the major local utility company, Key Bank's Dayton district, and Sinclair Community College, as well as the provost of Wright State University. The editorial board of the *Dayton Daily News* endorsed the project. Initially, school board members were also well disposed. Board member Clayton R. Luckie II said at the time, "Anything to bring up the scores, to bring up children's educational level."[17] In a 2008 interview for this book, Williams explained that "parents were tired of failing schools and they were looking for a solution. We lobbied the state to allow us to do conversion charters. . . . I had several schools that were just not performing. I wanted to convert those to charter schools."[18]

Short-Sighted Victory for the Status Quo

The day after Williams formally presented the plan to the school board, the Dayton Education Association (DEA) came out with guns blazing. Its president, Joyce Fulwiler Shawhan, vowed to fight any effort to turn over school operations to a for-profit firm. At a rally, she told teachers that their union would not stand for a "corporate takeover by a New York company."[19] Ohio Education Association president Michael Billirakis sought to veto any deal to turn over control of troubled DPS schools to outsiders. He told the *Dayton Daily News*, "We will not sit down and discuss options with an organization or a corporation whose primary objective is to destroy public education. . . . We've known for a number of years that the private sector sees a major bonanza in getting into public enterprises, in ripping money off."[20] In 2008, Williams recalled that "the NEA and the AFT sent in their heavy hitters to oppose the charter idea, and they were so effective that the school board would eventually refuse to endorse the plan."[21]

Yet Williams did his utmost, relentlessly reiterating four basic points to dozens of groups across the community:

- The Dayton public schools, like most urban districts in America, were failing too many children and needed a serious jolt of competition and innovation.
- It was in the district's interest to embrace charters rather than have them imposed by outsiders. Through the use of conversion charters, the district could control their quality and growth—and enjoy the support of the business community, higher education, and many civic leaders.
- To inveigh against for-profit operators was to misunderstand how public education works. Williams pointed out that "everything we do in education is for profit. Every penny I spend, someone is making a dollar off it—text books, computers, salaries for employees."[22]
- People who don't perform should be held accountable. Williams was blunt: "I've always said that until we hit people in the pocketbooks and for performance, nothing is going to change in urban education."[23]

Opponents countered that this was a corporate takeover of public education; that profits would come before the needs of children; that charters would siphon money away from the district; that the superintendent was really the problem (if he did his job, the district wouldn't have such woes); that the district should work with the union to fix its current schools; that the reconstitution plan would worsen the quality of public education and weaken local control; and, finally, that this was an experiment in which black children were being used as guinea pigs. Jessie O. Gooding, president of the Dayton Branch of the NAACP, asked the *Dayton Daily News*, "Why did they select only inner city schools—because [they're] predominantly black?"[24]

Similar arguments would be raised repeatedly by both sides in charter school debates over the next decade, at the statehouse, in federal and state courtrooms, in newspaper pages, and in the public square. In Dayton, though, the conversion-charter debate came to an abrupt end in late April 1998, when the teachers union voted overwhelmingly not to accept any changes to its collective bargaining agreement with the district. This effectively blocked Williams's effort to negotiate an operating agreement with Edison because Edison insisted that its teachers work longer days and years. In announcing the vote, the DEA's Shawhan declared, "We're a public school system and we shouldn't be managed by for-profit companies."[25]

To Williams, this was a defeat for children that would likely result in the district losing students to charter schools. But he also understood that it was a long-term defeat for teachers since the loss of students would eventually mean layoffs. He presciently told the *Dayton Daily News* that "when I have to lay off teachers, I'm going to lose my younger teachers because seniority prevails. I'm going to lose the future of education in this community. That's a shame."[26]

Looking back on this time, Williams lamented in 2008 that "at the end of the day, the union vetoed it. It was the biggest disappointment in my career."[27] He was not surprised to learn that the number of union teachers in DPS dropped from 2,000 in 1998 to 1,100 in 2008. "As enrollment declines," he explained, "districts lose money on per-pupil funding. Decline in enrollment, you have to lay off younger teachers. That's the trend across the country. You lose the best and brightest and those that are looking to change the culture. They're getting laid off and are going on to do something else. We blew it."[28]

The school board fired Williams in June 1999 amid news of a surprising $22.8 million deficit uncovered by a state audit. In announcing the findings, State Auditor Jim Petro warned that "this school district's financial condition is treacherous."[29] Along with Williams departed all serious talk of real partnerships between charter schools and the district for at least half a decade. His exit also chilled relations between the district and Dayton's business community. And it made clear to all just how hostile the system and, especially, its teachers' union were to real reform. This sentiment was captured by the *Dayton Daily News* when it editorialized that "Dayton teachers' decision last week to refuse to allow the Edison Project to manage charter schools was sad. . . . The failure to work something out worsens cynicism about public education generally and especially schools and teachers in Dayton. The damage to the union and to the community's reputation as a good place to live and do business will be long lasting. But the vote also was a measure of how scared the teachers are about their futures and changes—let's not mince words—that threaten them."[30] As Williams predicted, the union's vote opened the door to an explosion of start-up charter schools in Dayton, all of them nonunion. By the mid-2000s, Dayton had more children (per capita) enrolled in charters than any city in the country save for posthurricane New Orleans. Some of these schools were decent, some were mediocre and some were downright abysmal, but they nearly all drew pupils away from the Dayton public schools. It was clear that the system had lost the confidence of much of the city's population, and in just ten years Dayton would become a veritable bazaar of school choice, a dramatic change that would turn out to be fraught with problems of its own.

Notes

1. Scott Stephens, "Charter Schools Sorely Test Dayton," *Cleveland Plain Dealer*, May 21, 2001, 1A.
2. James A. Williams, "The Choice Is Transformation: Education for a New Generation," *Dayton Public Schools*, January 1, 1998, 10–11.
3. Ron Budzik, interview by Mike Lafferty, June 12, 2008.
4. Stephens, "Charter Schools."
5. *School Vouchers: Publicly Funded Programs in Cleveland and Milwaukee*, U.S. General Accounting Office, Report to the Honorable Judd Gregg, United States Senate, August 2001, 3.
6. Anita D. Suda and others, "Education Reform in the Dayton Area: Public Attitudes and Opinions," Thomas B. Fordham Foundation, October 1, 1998.
7. Lynn Hulsey, "Plan Gives Choice," *Dayton Daily News*, October 1, 1997, 1B.
8. Ibid.
9. Lynn Hulsey, "Private Effort Starts," *Dayton Daily News*, November 26, 1997, 2B.
10. Editorial, "Vouchers Not Substitute for Good Schools," *Dayton Daily News*, December 1, 1997, 6A.
11. Scott Elliott, "Group Helps Families Pay for School Choice," *Dayton Daily News*, April 5, 2008, 1A.
12. Scott Elliott, "10 Years Ago, PACE Sparked Change in Dayton," *Dayton Daily News*, April 4, 2008, http://www.daytondailynews.com/blogs/content/shared-gen/blogs/dayton/education/entries/2008/04/04/10_years_ago_pa.html.
13. Paul E. Peterson, "Vouchers Raise Black Students' Test Scores," National Center for Policy Analysis, *Executive Alert*, July–August 2002, 8.
14. William G. Howell, Patrick J. Wolf, Paul E. Peterson, and David E. Campbell, *Test-Score Effects of School Vouchers in Dayton, Ohio, New York City, and Washington, DC: Evidence from Randomized Field Trials* (Cambridge, MA: Harvard University, Kennedy School of Government, 2000), 4.
15. James A. Williams, *Re-Creating the Learning Community: A Proposal to Reconstitute Five Schools*, White Paper, Dayton Public Schools, December 30, 1997, 2.
16. Lynn Hulsey, "Williams Pushes Charter Proposal," *Dayton Daily News*, January 8, 1998, 1A.
17. Lynn Hulsey, "School May Privatize," *Dayton Daily News*, December 19, 1997, 1A.
18. James Williams, interview by Mike Lafferty, April 2008.
19. Lynn Hulsey, "Teachers Union Blasts For-Profits," *Dayton Daily News*, February 10, 1998, 2B.
20. Editorial, "Educators Debate Edison Project," *Dayton Daily News*, February 26, 1998, 11A.
21. Williams, interview.
22. Ibid.
23. Ibid.

24. Wendy Hundley and Mark Fisher, "NAACP Doubts Charter Plans," *Dayton Daily News*, April 10, 1998, 6B.

25. Lynn Hulsey, "Teachers Vote against Change," *Dayton Daily News*, April 23, 1998, 1B.

26. Ibid.

27. Williams, interview.

28. Ibid.

29. James Hannah, "Ohio Auditor: Dayton Schools Face Intervention," *Cincinnati Enquirer*, May 25, 1999, http://www.enquirer.com/editions/1999/05/25/loc_ohio_auditor_dayton.html.

30. Editorial, "Teachers' Vote Shows Division That Has to End," *Dayton Daily News*, April 27, 1998, 8A.

verything in sight, and the longer they're there, the harder it's going to e to move them out and away from the table."[4]

He recognized, of course, as did all charter foes, that the more of these chools that were launched, the more children attending them and the lon- er they existed, the more difficult it would be even to contain this form f competition, much less to eradicate it. With total school enrollments atic in Ohio and all the urban districts except Columbus shrinking, every oungster who opted for a charter school meant some $6,000 less into chool system coffers. Reduced budgets and enrollments also meant fewer aching jobs—and union dues.

It's no surprise that the establishment pushed back hard. What's more urprising is that Ohio's feisty charter movement did such a poor job of efending itself and solving the bona fide problems—particularly the edu- ation-quality problem—that eased the task of its foes. Charter schools in very state had critics and political enemies, but those in some jurisdic- ons—California and Colorado come immediately to mind—did far bet- r at policing themselves, recruiting influential allies, making their case, nd striking back at their foes.

An Argument against Itself

ormer House Speaker Jon Husted, one of Ohio's strongest and most influ- ntial charter supporters, recalled the fracas in a 2008 interview: "Every- ing from teachers to what I call the education spending lobby didn't want ompetition, and they worked hard to tarnish the image of school choice."[5] harter supporters also erred in trusting to market forces—parents exit- g bad schools—to repair or terminate weak schools. Along the way, they sisted realistic suggestions for greater oversight and confused legislators ith their inability to work together. As State Senator Jeff Jacobson also oted in 2008, "The charter movement has in many ways been the best gument against itself."[6]

From the start, Fordham worked with charter allies statewide—the hio Business Roundtable, David Brennan, former lawmaker Sally Perz, arious school operators, and other philanthropists—to build a viable atewide charter school organization that would not only promote and efend charters before legislators and jurists but also push a quality agenda r the schools themselves. Nevertheless, this effort proved impossible, ecause of the balkanized nature of the state's charter program. It was ever a single happy family or unified team—and no one tent seemed able contain it. Its contending interests included large and small for-profit anagement firms, nonprofit management organizations, scads of one-off

4

Be Careful What You Wish For

Once the charter fuse was lit in Dayton and Ohio's other major cit- ies, these schools exploded, much as happened in other states that allowed relatively unfettered charter programs. In a decade, the Buckeye State's version of charter schooling ballooned from fifteen such schools to more than 330, with enrollments rising to more than eighty-five thou- sand youngsters—some 4 percent of all students. As the law was written, charters were largely confined to urban Ohio—also home to many of the neediest youngsters—and in some communities it had a profound impact. Dayton, for example, went from a single charter school (with sixty-five pupils) in 1998 to thirty-four (and about 6,500 students) a decade later.

Quantity versus Quality

The rapid growth attested to inner-city parents' pent-up frustration and demand for alternatives to traditional district schools. But much of that expansion in Ohio and other rapid-growth jurisdictions took place with scant attention to academic quality. Some of the people and organizations that launched schools in Ohio were ill prepared. Some had eccentric views of what a school should be. Some operators turned out to be more inter- ested in personal enrichment than in delivering high-quality instruction to poor kids.

And what might, in hindsight, have been anticipated is exactly what happened: too many of the early charters failed to deliver acceptable aca- demic results. That's not what their supporters expected—or promised. Indeed, charter advocates in Ohio as elsewhere had set themselves a high bar. They had declared that these new schools would deliver academic results superior to traditional district schools—and they implied that this could happen with less money.

Indeed, in their ardor to launch the charter program, they had cut corners on resources. Whether proponents truly thought their schools could succeed on a relative shoestring or simply felt obliged to compromise with opponents fearful that charters would rifle district treasuries, Ohio's charter program began on extralean rations—leaner than in most other states.

The new schools received the same state and federal dollars per pupil as district-operated schools but they lacked access to significant local resources, including receipts from property and local sales tax revenues— all the supplemental funding that districts raise for themselves on top of monies sent from Columbus. This meant that Ohio charters were forced to operate with about 30 percent less money per pupil than district schools. Nor did they receive any public dollars for facilities, which meant they had to beg, borrow, lease, or try—on another shoestring—to buy space in which to teach their students. They used donated facilities, cut deals with inner-city churches, took over mothballed school buildings, rented store fronts, or—occasionally—built their own places with private capital.[1]

New charter schools could receive up to $450,000 in federal start-up dollars, and another $50,000 in state dollars.[2] Yet those funds could not be used for facilities. This meant that many start-up schools felt flush at the beginning, but these extra dollars vanished after the third year and charter revenues were thereafter based on tight per-pupil funding formulae. In effect, enrollments drove school budgets.

In retrospect, charters were being asked to make education bricks—better bricks than district schools—without enough straw. Located in the state's most troubled neighborhoods and enrolling youngsters least well served by the traditional schools of those communities, they were shouldering enormous education challenges without adequate resources and, too often, without adequate know-how, preparation, or external quality control.

When they didn't produce solid academic results, or otherwise messed up, their shortcomings were exposed by eager journalists and blasted by editorial writers. Headlines such as "Charters Fail to Deliver, Analysis Shows," "State Audit Says Charter School Company Owes Thousands," and "Wild Experiment" were ubiquitous. A few early horror stories grabbed a lot of attention. The Riser Academy, which opened in Columbus in 1999, was troubled from the outset, plagued by unfinished construction and a dearth of computers, textbooks, and other teaching materials, according to a review by State Auditor Petro. Its enrollment was overstated. Its management was accused of misspending state funds and the school was closed in 2000. But similar stories played out in every major Ohio city.

Fiscal outrages made for vivid headlines but the broader p too many Ohio charters was anemic academic results, well t averages. In June 2000, the *Cleveland Plain Dealer* reported tha school students did worse on the mandatory exams than young academically distressed districts from which they fled. . . . Stat five percent of charter-school students who took the fourth-g ciency test in March passed all five parts, compared to a 31% p for public schools. Just three percent passed the sixth-grade test to 35% for public schools."[3]

Again with the benefit of hindsight, we can see that some of t experienced by Ohio charter schools stemmed from decisions m made, at the start. From the get-go, charters were seen as a parti lican creation foisted on traditional school districts that—in board members, superintendents, and unions—simply neede hand from the state in the form of more money. Instead, they to swallow a gag-inducing dose of competition.

These and other foes began counterattacking immediatel sage of the first charter school bills, and the problems that su surfaced in the media furnished them with additional weap against these upstart institutions. Every year since 1998, bills introduced (by Democratic legislators) aimed at curtailing the charter schools and saddling them with additional costs and burdens. The Ohio Education Association, the Ohio Federatio ers, and their allies have also filed innumerable court challeng at charter schools. (One case eventually made it to the Ohi Court, which, in late 2006, narrowly—four to three—deemed program constitutional.)

Charter schools have also been targets of a relentless and w public relations campaign, particularly aimed at for-profit op White Hat, the company formed by David Brennan to run a schools. The teacher unions teamed up with the League of W ers, the Ohio PTA, the Ohio School Boards Association, an AFL-CIO to form "The Coalition for Public Education," wh distributed 173,000 copies of a flyer decrying "Public Educatic The statewide mailing termed the charter program "an acade ter" riddled with "allegations of fraud, gross mismanagem enrollment claims and misappropriated funds." The vitriolic interested—tone of the attacks was illustrated in 2003 by th of the Cleveland Teachers Union, Richard DeColibus. In a his union's $70,000 "truth" campaign, DeColibus declared bad [charter] schools are like 700-pound hogs at the dinner t

"mom-and-pop" schools, competing sponsors of many different kinds, philanthropists, and general school-reform types who supported this version of choice.

Some trusted the parent marketplace and hewed to a laissez-faire approach to school growth and quality, while others—Fordham was squarely in this camp—insisted that charters needed to deliver better academic results than district schools.

Indeed, some key players in Ohio's charter movement resented Fordham because they saw our focus on school effectiveness as naively idealistic; insulated by our endowment and enveloped by theory, they thought, we didn't adequately understand business or sufficiently trust markets—and we jeopardized their own efforts to grow and be left alone.

This tension manifested itself in the emergence of two separate state charter organizations—the Ohio Charter School Association (OCSA) and the Ohio Community Schools Center (OCSC). Such divisions made for weak, sparring lobbying efforts and befuddled lawmakers, a pattern that continued throughout the saga of Ohio's charter school program. Fordham provided funding and support to the OCSC and worked with partners to develop a merger of these two faltering groups into one stronger entity.

That took place in 2003, but the consolidated organization perished two years later. We knew the handwriting was on the wall when we realized that—with total contributions of less than $100,000—little Fordham was the group's largest single donor. All the state's deep-pocketed philanthropies kept their distance—a worrisome sign of the pariah status that charter schools enjoyed across the Ohio establishment (and a worrisome sign for Ohio of how establishment aversion to education boat rocking would slow the pace of reform in a place that sorely needed more of it faster).

In 2006, two charter school groups again emerged in Ohio. With leadership from the National Alliance for Public Charter Schools, encouragement by Fordham, and financial support from several of America's largest procharter foundations (but no serious Buckeye donors!), the Ohio Alliance for Public Charter Schools sought to be the unified, umbrella advocacy group that the state's charter movement sorely needed and it pledged allegiance to the quality and results that the movement needed even worse. But its capacity to speak for the entire movement was swiftly end-run by another new group calling itself the Ohio Coalition for Quality Education. Both spoke to lawmakers and journalists on behalf of charter schools and charter policy, adding further to the confusion and balkanization. (A third group, called School Choice Ohio, at first thought it would lobby on charter issues as well as vouchers but gradually came to focus exclusively on the latter.)

We opted to invest modest sums of Fordham dollars in the Ohio Alliance for Public Charter Schools but sought to maintain cordial relationships with both groups, as well as with School Choice Ohio. We also provided modest support for the efforts of School Choice Ohio, and we shared intelligence, ideas, and strategic information with the leaders of all three organizations. Still and all, among the crippling weaknesses that have dogged the Ohio charter venture since day one is its continuing failure to come together under a single flag or agree upon a single, coherent policy agenda that places the interests of children first. As with the public education establishment itself, adult interests somehow always take precedence.

Another frailty besetting charter schools in Ohio—and across the land—was the movement's (and policymakers') weak understanding of how actually to hold these new schools to account for their results. Few appreciated the importance, or even the function, of authorizers (known in Ohio as sponsors) in regulating the charter market and ensuring academic quality.[7] Done right, authorizers' responsibilities include carefully vetting would-be school operators for competence, sincerity, and plausibility; closing nonperforming schools; strengthening decent ones; and seeking out strong new schools to open.

Unfortunately, Ohio's early sponsors, notably including the state's own department of education, did a poor job of encouraging good prospective operators to enter the market or screening out unpromising candidates. They didn't discriminate much at all. Pretty much everyone who applied for a school charter got one, a "wild west" atmosphere that may have been suited to states like Arizona (which had America's fastest-growing charter program) but was anathema in more staid locales like Massachusetts and New York (both of which have far smaller charter programs with far fewer quality problems). According to State Auditor Jim Petro, "the problem was that the [Ohio] Department [of Education] did nothing to investigate the applications (for running a school), and they would approve charters with little analysis because they were under political pressure to do so."[8]

Once new schools launched, Ohio authorizers did little to monitor their academic performance or intervene in those with weak results. By far the state's largest authorizer in the early days, the Ohio Department of Education (ODE) was assiduous about regulatory compliance and bureaucratic T-crossing but nearly oblivious to academic achievement. Indeed, it seemed only to awaken to its sponsorship obligations when one or another of the schools it sponsored got into serious media trouble that threatened to embarrass the agency.

There was reason for this lackadaisical attitude, Petro declared: "ODE staff could have cared less about charter schools. These staffers came from public schools and they bought into the argument of money being siphoned away"[9] from district schools. He was, of course, suggesting that the authorizer itself would be just as happy if this unsought responsibility were to go away and this irksome, threatening new breed of schools were to vanish. Ohio's other big sponsor, the Lucas County Education Service Center, was also promiscuous in granting charters, earning Husted's later admonishment. "They tarnished the charter-school movement by sponsoring bad schools," he said.[10] In short, in the early days of the program, quantity trounced quality, and accountability was more notional than real.

But it's not hard to see what was happening. Advocates pressed for growth, confident that this was good for the children who would immediately benefit from more charter capacity and also that the more schools and students that entered the charter vehicle the more political traction it would acquire. If it got large enough, went the reasoning, nobody would ever dare to shut it down. Operators naturally benefited from this approach—and parents responded. Often desperate for safe, welcoming alternatives for their children, thousands of families enrolled their youngsters in Ohio's dozens of new charter schools without much regard to their academic program, organizational competence, or track record.

This worried us. As early as September 1998, Fordham's Finn and Mike Petrilli warned in an op-ed in the *Columbus Dispatch* that the "state's fledgling community [charter] schools program already is stumbling into an avoidable trap: accountability problems."[11] They observed that ODE felt "compelled to grant a charter to every applicant. . . . This lack of selectivity and persnicketiness is practically unheard of nationally, and is a worrisome precedent for Ohio. . . . These schools need to be held to ambitious academic standards and judged by measurable results, not just their marketplace appeal. They should set a precedent for conventional public schools by showing that, with the benefit of independence, it's indeed possible to produce far better results than most regular schools are doing, particularly for poor and minority youngsters."[12] Nevertheless, far from preaching to the choir, ours was more like a lonesome voice in the wilderness.

Repair Efforts

What happened in the Ohio legislature by the early 2000s was often determined by Jon Husted, who, as house speaker from 2005 to 2009, largely shaped the legislative agenda. Husted earned his bachelor's and master's degrees in education from the University of Dayton in the late 1980s and was an all-American football player in 1989. In the 1990s, he served as vice president of the Dayton Area Chamber of Commerce. When elected to the

Ohio House in 2000, representing suburban Kettering, Husted immediately became a serious force in the legislature.

Husted shared the view that charter schools could provide competition to inner-city schools as well as outlets for parents and children who wanted out of failing schools. He believed in choice and markets. But he also believed in academic performance. And, in 2002, when Petro blasted ODE's handling of its charter responsibilities, he took the lead in reforming Ohio's charter law.

The auditor's review of the charter program was conducted after eight schools closed for financial mismanagement and left taxpayers on the hook for several million dollars.[13] But problems were not limited to that particular octet. For example, Ohio had paid a "virtual" charter school[14] $1.7 million for students who weren't even enrolled. The state couldn't make the school refund the money because ODE had not established adequate guidelines for counting charter students and funding their schools.

In an interview before his audit was released, Petro told the *Dispatch* that "there were no findings for recovery [against the school] because in September and October [of 2000] there was no description of what DOE (Department of Education) expected. It is an example of how to botch the establishment of a new charter school."[15] Petro said he believed that the school, Electronic Classroom of Tomorrow, or ECOT, was gaming the system. "ECOT counted anyone who signed up, even if someone called in or the school called someone back. Cha-ching. You get paid for that,"[16] Petro said. (ECOT remains in business today, enrolling some 7,000 students at an annual cost to Ohio taxpayers of approximately $50 million.)

Petro's comprehensive review made clear that charter schools had grown rapidly without enough attention to quality control: "Ohio, like other Charter School Law states, has encountered implementation problems in developing its community (charter) school program. In some cases, unrealistic expectations have created an environment for school failure. In other cases, statutory improvements need to be made in the areas of facilities, transportation, and monitoring and oversight. Some community school operators are unprepared to run an organization of the size and complexity of a public school, particularly on the business side."[17] Petro also blasted ODE for its lackluster oversight of the state's charter schools. Indeed, he recommended that the agency "improve its performance within two months or risk losing oversight of the independent public schools."[18] He suggested that lawmakers consider either establishing an independent commission to sponsor charters or broadening the sponsor pool beyond ODE and delegate more authority to independent sponsors. He particularly wanted big-city districts to get into sponsorship as well as universities and colleges, which he believed would have resources to monitor and advise their schools.[19] Petro and his team had little confidence in ODE's ability both to serve as a charter sponsor and to provide schools with needed technical assistance and professional support. As he noted, associating with charters was the last thing the department's careerists wanted. Many legislators shared Petro's view. Husted captured their concerns when he said, "I knew that our community schools law and the enforcement of that law were inadequate to the point that we were setting many schools up for failure."[20] By March 2002, he had filed a bill to overhaul the charter law. It incorporated many of Petro's 109 recommendations, including ending ODE's direct sponsorship duties. "You can't be the cheerleader and the referee at the same time," he said in an interview in 2008.[21] Husted's bill, a copy of which he displayed on his office wall while he was speaker, completely redesigned charter school oversight in the Buckeye State—and, in retrospect, caused almost as many new problems as it solved.

As enacted in January 2003, House Bill 364 reshaped the charter landscape. It revamped and strengthened operational procedures and financial reporting, while making it harder for greedy operators to scam the state. "While not particularly glamorous, these fundamental aspects of the system are phenomenally better than they were in the past," argued Steve Burigana, the education department official responsible for overseeing charter schools at the time.[22] The act called on new schools to be sponsored by districts, county educational service centers,[23] state universities, and nonprofit 501(c)3 corporations that met certain minimum requirements.[24]

Additionally, new charter sponsors had to be approved by the ODE and had to negotiate a performance contract with that agency before they could take on the duties of authorizing. "These are community schools," noted Husted, as he explained the rationale for multiple and diverse sponsors. "We want people to sponsor them who are from the community, who have a stake in their success." He also argued that House Bill 364 would "restore the integrity of the charter-school system and increase the ways to hold it accountable."[25]

We at Fordham had extensively studied quality sponsorship around the country, believed in the merits of having multiple authorizers from which would-be school operators could seek charters, and generally viewed the new law as a positive development, particularly its shift of sponsorship responsibility away from ODE. Writing in the *Dayton Daily News*, we noted,

> though charter schools themselves are under a microscope, not enough attention has been paid to the seriousness with which the "sponsors" hold up their end of the relationship. Looking around the country, we see some sponsors that are too bureaucratic and others that are too lax. In Ohio, as

elsewhere, too many sponsors have viewed their job as giving birth to a school and then abandoning it to make its way in the world alone.

That was the gist of State Auditor Jim Petro's critical report on charter schools. Now that the Ohio Department of Education is becoming, in effect, the authorizer of authorizers, it must take pains to define and carry out this role. Nowhere is this more important than in determining which nonprofit organizations will win the right to open charter schools.[26]

Not all charter supporters shared our hope for the new chartering regime. Sally Perz, for one, had always wanted an independent, statewide sponsor running the program but she wasn't happy with ODE either as an authorizer or as—now—the sponsor of sponsors. As she told a newspaper reporter, "The irony is that the largest sponsor in the state—and not necessarily the premier sponsor—will now have oversight over sponsors. It's ludicrous. It's a mismatch to the core. They are the ultimate bureaucracy."[27]

Unintended Consequences

While solving some problems, Husted's reforms also brought unintended consequences. One was that the seventy-nine charter schools sponsored by ODE needed to find other sponsors by June 30, 2005, or else close. A new sponsorship sector had to be created from scratch in about two years—with no funds from the general assembly. Nor were all the extant authorizers placed under ODE's oversight. Some were grandfathered in, including traditional school districts, the Lucas County Educational Service Center (sponsor of the ECOT school), and the University of Toledo's (UT's) Ohio Council of Community Schools. They would remain accountable to nobody in particular.

Although the advantages of multiple sponsors within a state is an article of doctrinal faith across the American charter movement, it carries risks, too, and all of them would eventually manifest themselves in Ohio. The teacher unions and other elements of the public school establishment invariably want to restrict charter sponsorship to traditional districts—and charter advocates invariably oppose that constraint on grounds that it leaves the fox in command of the chicken coop and empowers the existing monopoly to block unwanted competition. Charter doctrine insists that a state will have a livelier, more diverse, more robust, and more competitive charter sector if would-be operators can bring their plans to various sponsors or—at minimum—appeal their rejection by local school districts.

What the charter bible doesn't quite make clear is to whom the multiple authorizers are themselves accountable other than themselves. When a school system sponsors charter schools, it can be held to account by its own electorate, mayor, or other local governance arrangement. State agencies are eventually accountable to governor and legislature and, through them, to voters. But what about universities? "Independent" chartering bodies? And nonprofit groups that normally answer only to their own trustees?

House Bill 364 addressed part of that problem when it made new sponsors accountable to ODE (while taking the risk that concerned Sally Perz—that ODE would handle this as badly as it had handled its own sponsorship), but neglected part of it by grandfathering in a number of extant authorizers, including the state's two largest.

At first, though, we were less troubled by the proliferation of sponsors than by their dearth and, in particular, by the challenge of finding enough good sponsors to keep orphaned schools from closing. In response, we moved to launch what became known as the Ohio Charter School Sponsor Institute, in partnership with ODE and the National Association of Charter School Authorizers. It was financed by the state ($500,000), the Walton Family Foundation ($250,000), and the Bill and Melinda Gates Foundation ($250,000). Its mission was to identify, recruit, and train community-focused and results-driven charter school sponsors, especially qualified nonprofit organizations and colleges and universities.[28]

The importance of this effort was spelled out in a memo from the Fordham staff to board members in May 2003:

> Ohio urgently needs high-performing charter schools. Abuse or incompetence by new sponsors will put students at risk and endanger Ohio's (and the nation's) charter movement. It is also unlikely that suitable sponsors will spontaneously come forward in sufficient number and with sufficient knowledge and capacity to meet the needs of Ohio's program.
>
> The opportunity, therefore, is for Ohio to "get sponsorship right." The significance of this opportunity reaches far beyond the Buckeye State. Minnesota law already allows 501(c)3 organizations to sponsor schools and a bill recently under consideration in California would do likewise. By building effective new sponsors "from scratch," Ohio can design and implement effective authorizer models for dissemination and replication in other states. The stakes are pretty high so we have decided to put ourselves right in the middle of this project.[29]

John Rothwell led the institute. At one time, he had overseen ODE's charter school efforts as well as those of the Cincinnati public schools. (A few years earlier, that city's superintendent, Steven Adamowski, was a reformer who embraced charter schools as part of the district's makeover strategy, but he was eventually defeated by the teachers union after bitter fights with his board over merit pay.) Rothwell canvassed the state in search of leading nonprofit organizations, as well as colleges and universities, ready to serve as sponsors, but found few takers. In October 2003 he reported that "most clearly communicate either no interest or grave concerns about charter school sponsorship."[30]

These organizations voiced worries about legal liability and costs, as well as the politics of taking on this role in a state whose public school establishment despised charters and everything associated with them. Although attorneys indicated that the liability risk could be contained,[31] potential sponsors remained jittery. They found ample excuses to remain on the sidelines, including potential costs to their reputations and pocketbooks. In 2003, the constitutionality of Ohio's charter school program was being challenged by state and federal lawsuits. Seldom did a week pass without bad press for charter schools. Some poor operators had tarnished the movement. Some of them, Husted recalled, either weren't qualified or had motives that were not "pure."

The treacherous political environment discouraged both nonprofit groups and state universities from venturing into the ill-mapped territory of sponsorship. In fact, just as House Bill 364 was becoming law, UT's trustees voted to end its direct sponsorship efforts, apparently under threats from charter opponents, including local school districts that—outrageously—said they would not hire UT-trained teachers if the university did not foreswear its complicity with this hated "reform."

The economics of sponsorship were also daunting. It was unclear what this work would actually cost, what personnel would be needed to do it at all, much less do it well, and what kind of a market for schools would exist. Additionally, it wasn't clear whether the schools would actually be willing to pay "sponsorship fees." Underfunded to begin with, they had been getting free sponsorship from ODE and were now being asked to pay for it. The only way authorizers could support themselves was from fees levied on the schools they sponsored. The new law set those fees at up to 3 percent of a school's per-pupil funding. Some schools considered this a tax and didn't like the idea of paying thousands of dollars to an organization to hold them accountable and possibly even close them for underperformance. Nor was it crystal clear what the day-to-day duties of sponsors actually consisted of. Only when one started to negotiate a contract with ODE did the full and formidable list of responsibilities begin to emerge.

By late 2003, nearly a year after enactment of the charter reform law, no high-quality organizations had stepped up as sponsor for Dayton's existing armada of charter schools. Business leaders and charter supporters asked whether Fordham had any interest in taking this on. Our initial answer was no. We were a think tank. Actually getting our hands dirty wasn't what we did. Nevertheless, by early 2004, as few qualified nonprofits offered themselves as authorizers, the foundation began to reconsider. We worried that decent charter schools would be orphaned when ODE left the sponsorship business and, unable to obtain new sponsors, would be forced to close. Still, both staff and board were cautious. Ohio's charter marketplace was changing rapidly. It was a lot like walking on a trampoline. Had we known just how bouncy it would become, we might have been even more hesitant.

In evaluating the efforts of the Ohio Charter School Sponsor Institute in the summer of 2005, Western Michigan University analyst Louann Bierlein Palmer described the charter school/sponsorship marketplace that evolved in Ohio from 2003 to 2005. She noted that the organizations grandfathered in as sponsors had significant competitive advantages. She observed that as

the law change [in H.B. 364] removed sponsorship responsibilities from the State Board, it left in place such rights for the Lucas County Educational Service Center (ESC), the Ohio Council of Community Schools, and the Cincinnati, Cleveland, and Dayton Public Schools. Each of these entities, as well as all traditional district school boards, could continue sponsoring schools without seeking approval from the State Department. All other eligible entities (i.e., vocational school districts, other county education service centers, public universities and colleges, and nonprofit organizations) needed to obtain approval from the state prior to sponsoring a new start-up charter school or taking over the sponsorship of an existing school.[32]

In practice, this meant the grandfathered sponsors had a two-year window in which to open new schools and sign contracts with existing schools with no competition from new sponsors. According to Professor Palmer, this resulted in a sponsorship market very different from what was intended under the new law. She observed, "The original intent of that law was to have a number of active sponsors available to support community schools within their geographic region, and that there would not necessarily be competition between sponsors for schools. Thus there was an interest in finding at least one eligible entity willing to take on a sponsorship role within each of Ohio's metropolitan areas."

Yet, Palmer continued,

the notion of community-based noncompetitive sponsors quickly changed when Lucas County ESC, which under the previous law had been sponsoring only about 10 schools in the Toledo area, decided to take their chartering role statewide (by placing a representative within 50 miles of each charter school they sponsored). Given their existing infrastructure, Lucas County ESC began charging a sponsorship fee much smaller than the three percent allowed by law (usually one percent per pupil). And since Lucas County ESC and the Ohio Council of Community Schools were the only two existing non-district sponsors allowed to open schools from January 2003 to July 1, 2005, a large number of schools entered into contracts with these sponsors. As of May 2005, Lucas County ESC had 112 operating schools, with 70 additional signed contracts.[33]

And that feeding frenzy would likely continue. Lucas County ESC was using its advantage as a grandfathered sponsor to become the dominant charter authorizer in the state. On its current trajectory, it would grow, in less than two years, from being a local sponsor of fewer than a dozen charter schools around Toledo to America's largest sponsor. This was reckless, craven, and, for Ohio's charter movement, damaging. The ESC hastily issued dozens of contracts to school operators that showed little evidence of knowing what they were doing.

By promiscuously handing out charters, Lucas County ESC made the same mistakes that ODE had previously made but on an even grander scale. For example, the operator of the Colin Powell Leadership Academy in Dayton, a K–5 school that had been rated "in academic emergency" (the equivalent of an F grade) by the state every year since its 2001 opening, was issued five more contracts by Lucas County in 2005 to open additional charter schools in Dayton and elsewhere. Such callous disregard for educational quality was part of what triggered calls by the Dayton public schools and the mayor of Dayton for a moratorium on new charter schools. It also raised hackles in the general assembly, littered the landscape with feeble schools that would plague the charter program for years to come, and ushered in still more changes to Ohio's rapidly complexifying charter law.

Notes

1. Sheree Speakman and others, *Charter School Funding: Inequity's Next Frontier,* Thomas B. Fordham Institute, Dayton, OH, August 2005, 106.
2. Ohio phased out its start-up support for charters in 2007.
3. Scott Stephens, "Charter Schools Don't Do Well on State Exams; Passage Rates Are Worse Than Public Schools," *Cleveland Plain Dealer,* June 27, 2000, 1B.
4. Richard DeColibus, quoted in "Cleveland Union President Delivers External and Internal Rants," Education Intelligence Agency, October 6, 2003, http://www.eiaonline.com/archives/20031006.htm.
5. Speaker Husted, interview by Mike Lafferty, June 11, 2008.
6. Senator Jacobson, interview by Mike Lafferty, June 12, 2008.
7. Here and throughout this volume we use the terms *authorizer* and *sponsor* interchangeably.

8. Former State Auditor and Attorney General Jim Petro, interview by Mike Lafferty, June 10, 2008.
9. Ibid.
10. Husted, interview.
11. Chester E. Finn, Jr., and Michael Petrilli, "Raise Bar for Newest 'Public Schools,'" *Columbus Dispatch*, September 12, 1998.
12. Ibid.
13. John Gehring, "Audit Spurs Drive to Revamp Ohio's Charter School System," *Education Week*, February 27, 2002, 14.
14. In Ohio, an e-school is a full-time online school in which students enroll and earn credit but work primarily from home on computers and through the Internet. E-schools in Ohio can educate students within a district, across districts, and statewide. In 2008, some thirty-two such schools enrolled approximately twenty-four thousand pupils.
15. Donna Glenn, "School Overpaid, Auditor Says," *Columbus Dispatch*, November 14, 2001, 1E.
16. Ibid.
17. Jim Petro, "Ohio Department of Education Community Schools Operational Review," *Auditor of State*, February 7, 2002, 1.
18. Gehring, "Audit Spurs Drive."
19. Petro, interview.
20. Ruth E. Sternberg, "Petro: Fix Charter Schools—Auditor Has 109 Ways to Improve Oversight," *Columbus Dispatch*, February 8, 2002, 1A.
21. Jon Husted, interviews by Lee Leonard, 2007, and Mike Lafferty, June 11, 2008.
22. Alexander Russo, "A Tough Nut to Crack in Ohio: Charter Schooling in the Buckeye State," Progressive Policy Institute, Washington, DC, February 2005, 11. http://www.ppionline.org/documents/Ohioreport_0201.pdf
23. Many other states have county-level education agencies that are typically charged with managing certain state programs, providing selected services to district schools, and, sometimes, operating specialized schools and those located in unincorporated areas.
24. These requirements included having been in operation for at least five years, having at least $500,000 in assets, and having an "education-oriented" mission. At this writing, Minnesota is the only other state to allow and encourage nonprofit organizations to sponsor charter schools.
25. Catherine Candisky, "Charter School Oversight May Change," *Columbus Dispatch*, March 20, 2002, 5B.
26. Chester E. Finn, Jr., and Terry Ryan, "Husted Bill an Important Step for Charters," *Dayton Daily News*, December 18, 2002.
27. Ruth E. Sternberg, "State Board Seeking Changes in Rules for Charter Schools," *Columbus Dispatch*, February 14, 2002, 6B.
28. Louann Bierlein Palmer, *Summative External Evaluation Report*, Ohio Charter School Sponsor Institute, Dayton, OH, August 4, 2005.
29. Terry Ryan, "Ohio Charter School Sponsor Institute," Memorandum to Thomas B. Fordham Institute Board of Trustees, May 28, 2003.

30. John Rothwell, e-mail to Sponsor Institute Advisory Board, October 1, 2003.

31. Chad A. Readler, "Community School Sponsors: Potential Liabilities and Possible Solutions," Jones Day Memorandum to Ohio Charter School Association, Dayton, OH, August 5, 2003.

32. Palmer, External Evaluation Report.

33. Ibid.

5

Urban School Reform

Part II

Home to the most charter schools in the state, the greatest proportion of charter students, and some of the charter movement's strongest supporters, Dayton has been ground zero for Ohio charters. In many ways, its saga is a microcosm of the state's and even the nation's experience with this distinctive urban school reform strategy. But charters weren't the only such strategy in Dayton; partly because of their influence, the school system itself began to show renewed signs of life.

Takeover of the Public Schools

In November 2001, a reform-minded slate of candidates won a majority of seats on Dayton's Board of Education. These four women were bent on giving the district a complete makeover. Voters were mightily frustrated with the district. Students and parents were deserting its schools and many families that could afford it simply moved out of town. If there was ever time for a major systemwide overhaul, it was now.

The quartet was led by the dynamic African American lawyer and businesswoman Gail Littlejohn, then a senior executive at the global online information provider LexisNexis. She ran for school board because she was dismayed by how poorly students in the Dayton public schools (DPS) were performing. Her own children were already in college. Wanting to make a difference, she first joined the board of Parents Advancing Choice in Education, or PACE. "That sort of planted the seed," she recalled in an interview for this book. "Everyone I talked to said it was darn near impossible [to improve the schools] and I get some energy about trying to do the impossible." She studied the issues, read books, especially those by

Frederick Hess, Paul Hill, and Donald McAdams. "All I needed was a glimmer of hope," she said.[1]

Flying a banner that said "Kids First," Littlejohn and her three compatriots made bold proposals and won wide support. Everyone understood that their goal was to win control of the seven-member school board, which for years had been a model of dysfunction and, even when in the grip of recent reform plans, wholly unable to counter the powerful teachers' union or overcome the district's own bureaucratic inertia.

The Kids First candidates said they welcomed charter school competition; emphasized the need to close underutilized schools; and declared that administrators and teachers had to be accountable.[2] This was heady stuff, and excited business leaders contributed over $200,000 to their campaign. This was an unheard-of sum for a Dayton school board election and contrasted with the paltry $13,000 raised by their five opponents.

Kids First swept to victory—further aided, almost everyone in Dayton agrees, by the widespread sense that this was the last chance to save the system from hemorrhaging to death—and from the beginning the foursome seemed serious about real change. "We raise the bar beginning this evening,"[3] Littlejohn declared as she was sworn in as the board's new president in January 2002. They hit the ground running. "We didn't have the luxury of trying to figure out what to do," she recalled. With academic challenges aplenty, a massive building levy campaign to win, and innumerable other goals, Littlejohn learned right away that leading this reform effort would be the most challenging mission she had ever undertaken.

Percy Mack, a new and relatively charismatic superintendent recruited by the new board majority, was an asset, but she also needed the Kids First election supporters to remain engaged. For example, she urgently needed to retain the business community's interest and support. Dayton's Business-Education Advisory Committee had been largely ignored by the previous board and its members were exasperated. "They [the committee] would give grants and they never knew what happened to the money," Littlejohn said.[4]

She and her team found a crumbling urban school system in which even the teachers seemed to have given up hope. Experts from the Council of the Great City Schools, invited to Dayton by Littlejohn, summed up the challenges faced by the district in a February 2002 report. Its opening paragraph declared that "the Dayton Public Schools are in crisis. Student achievement is low. Funding is tenuous. Buildings are dilapidated. And the public is clearly looking at options. Without change, parents will find or create them. The warning signs are everywhere."[5]

A sweeping indictment of DPS in its present state, the report listed five urgent challenges:

- DPS had the lowest achievement levels of any city in the state.[6]
- School enrollment was shrinking faster than that of any other major city system in America. Between 1990 and 2000, it dropped by a quarter to 21,000 pupils, a decline that accelerated after 1998 when the first Dayton charter opened.[7]
- There was a lack of public confidence and approbation. A Fordham-sponsored poll of Dayton parents showed that just 23 percent gave their public schools an A grade, while 16 percent conferred either a D or an F.
- The physical plant was decaying. The Great City Schools report noted that no new school had opened in Dayton in two decades. In consequence, nearly 27 percent of the district budget was devoted to building operations, utilities, maintenance, and repairs.[8]
- The desegregation plan was outdated. The district was still operating under one of America's oldest court-ordered desegregation plans, which weakened neighborhoods, undermined parental choice of schools, and eroded community support.[9]

Tackling multiple problems at once, the Kids First team chalked up some early wins. On April 15, 2002, the board, the NAACP, and the State of Ohio signed a history-making agreement that led federal judge Walter Rice to end twenty-six years of compulsory busing for purposes of racial balance. Under the settlement, DPS received $32.3 million from the state. That same day, the school system, the NAACP, and the area's three universities (Central State, the University of Dayton, and Wright State) issued a report entitled "Setting an Educational Reform Agenda for the Dayton Public Schools: A Call for Action and Change." It helped to convince Judge Rice that DPS was now serious about educating all the city's children.

The school board and district leaders had an ambitious set of priorities, above all boosting literacy and math achievement, elevating the quality of teachers and administrators, improving pupil behavior, and expanding preschool. Their agenda called, among many items, for the district to appoint a "reading czar" and for elementary pupils to spend two and a half hours every day on reading and writing. Staff development was to be aggressively pursued, the student conduct code revised, and penalties strengthened for weapons possession, violence, or threats.

Bricks and Mortar

Yet the board's first major project—ultimately a major distraction—involved bricks and mortar. Even before the ink was dry on their academic reform plan, board members were laying the groundwork for passage of a referendum authorizing a bond issue of $245 million to overhaul the district's buildings. Why would DPS rush to deal with the slow dilapidation of its physical plant when it had its work cut out halting the district's free fall into academic chaos? Just follow the money. Ohio was using its share of the multi-billion-dollar national tobacco settlement to help its school districts, especially needy urban and rural districts, pay for new buildings. In Dayton, the state would underwrite about 60 percent of an estimated $650 million school construction project. District leaders argued that "this is a once-in-a-lifetime opportunity to literally rebuild our schools."

That may well have been so, but it also meant the new board would spend much of its time, energy, and political capital during its first year in getting the construction levy passed. Which is indeed what happened: on November 5, 2002, Dayton voters approved a $245 million bond issue, which, when coupled with state contributions of nearly $400 million,[10] became one of the area's largest-ever public works projects.[11] Passing that levy was a feather in the DPS cap—but it also posed some tough questions.

For example: do new buildings make any difference in children's learning? District officials argued that "moving instruction from schools that average 67-years-old to new, state-of-the-art buildings will facilitate learning and help students improve their academic work."[12] Yet little evidence from other cities supported this claim. At the Fordham Foundation, we worried that a single-minded focus on facilities would inevitably blunt the district's commitment to academic achievement. We noted in a board memo that "this levy will turn out to be a mistake if it distracts the board, the system's executives or the community's leaders from the even more urgent academic priorities charted by the Great City Schools and incorporated in the district's strategic plan. And it could prove a major blunder if the bond issue campaign inadvertently signals to Daytonians that new buildings will cure what ails their schools."[13] Littlejohn disagreed that the building effort interfered with her other priorities, particularly boosting academics, which did improve for several years under her leadership. "I tried to keep them separate. I don't think passing the levy detracted from academics. . . . It was a short levy run. . . . I took a lead on the levy and the superintendent took a lead but everyone else was free to do their regular day jobs," she said.

A related early challenge was how to rightsize the district, given its shrinking pupil base. That included deciding which buildings should be replaced, which repaired, and which demolished, always thorny issues. "The community started arguing, do we shut down Roosevelt [High School]? Or build a new school?" Littlejohn noted. It was complicated stuff but she insisted that the construction plan did not dominate the board's agenda. "We didn't have all-day retreats talking about facilities but we did have all-day retreats talking about academics."[14]

In July 2003, education analyst Paul Hill, director of the University of Washington's Center on Reinventing Public Education, asked a Dayton gathering, "With all the changes in Dayton's school demographics—families moving around, kids moving from school to school, and Dayton proper contracting—how does the district know where families and children are actually going to be in 10-years time?" In fact, as noted by the Council of the Great City Schools, Dayton had seen its student enrollment drop by a quarter in a single decade. What evidence was there that this falloff would not continue during the next decade or even accelerate? The district basically answered, "If we build it, they will come [back]."

What galled and alienated charter school supporters was that not a single dollar of these millions for new buildings would benefit charter pupils, even though all businesses and parents in Dayton would pay higher taxes to support the construction. When the levy was passed in November 2002, about 18,100 students attended Dayton public schools and about 4,700 were enrolled in Dayton charter schools. By 2008, the district had contracted to just about 15,000 students while charters served some 6,500. The district's ongoing shrinkage, combined with meager academic improvement, suggested that Littlejohn and her associates were not particularly gifted prophets.

Collaboration?

Early on, the Kids First board members and charter school supporters worked together when they could. Business people who had supported the Kids First campaign also supported charter schools and believed that the new board members were truly focused on the needs of children as opposed to the interests of adults in the school system. In a national story on charter schools in April 2002, an *Education Week* reporter observed that "instead of viewing the newcomer [charter] schools as threats, or denying that they'd ever amount to much, district leaders now acknowledge that the migration by students to charters reflects some of the traditional public schools' own failings and compels them to improve."[15] Littlejohn agrees, up to a point. "Parents took advantage of charter competition . . . to shop for schools. That's what competition will do. If there is a competitor, they will go and see if they get better service," she said.[16]

Superintendent Percy Mack was already competing when, in August 2002, in one of his first speeches to Dayton educators, he noted that "our performance is better than the [other] choice. We must market our district like no other time in the history of Dayton. If we don't improve, we're going to have even less money. If each of us took on the drive and work ethic, we will bring students back to the Dayton Public Schools."[17]

In 2002 and 2003, district leaders talked seriously about working with charter schools, possibly even giving birth to a few of their own. In a bit of deal making designed to rally the business community behind the building levy campaign, the board agreed to create an academic charter high school. Its partners in this effort were the University of Dayton, the Gates Foundation, the Cincinnati-based KnowledgeWorks Foundation, and several local philanthropists, all led by University of Dayton education dean Tom Lasley. In August 2003, nine months after the levy was approved, DPS opened the Dayton Early College Academy (DECA).

The school began with about one hundred students. At the outset, it was a sort of hybrid, a district contract school, not a charter per se, although it would convert to charter status in 2007. It was housed on the university campus, although this came after a considerable internal struggle. University leaders were unsure that it was appropriate for a Catholic institution of higher education to operate a public high school, especially when local Catholic schools were closing themselves for lack of students. Yet the university had a strong commitment to training teachers for the inner city, and eventually the university board overcame its misgivings and embraced the new school. By 2009, DECA was one of Dayton's top-performing high schools.

For a time it seemed that DPS, too, might stretch beyond its traditional boundaries. Littlejohn, her colleagues on the board, and Mack spoke of forming district-charter partnerships, and Littlejohn pictured a charter-like "tight-loose" system in which schools would have greater autonomy to run themselves, contingent on doing a decent job of it.

There was even talk of bringing some extant charters into the district as "contract schools." They would embody a hybrid governance model that incorporates some of the charters' essential freedoms (e.g., to make curriculum, instructional, and at least some staffing decisions). But they would still be district schools and their funding would flow to the schools via DPS. Moreover, their staff would be employees of the DPS, which would limit the instructional pool to DPS teachers and fix their pay under the extant union contracts. The district did bring the freestanding World of Wonder charter school under its management with this sort of arrangement in

2006. Despite the hopeful talk, however, and notwithstanding what may have been a genuine desire, the district could not bring itself to "sponsor" full-fledged independent charter schools. The main reason was money. The prospect of bona fide collaboration between charters and DPS dimmed as the financial pain of losing students intensified. When a child leaves the district for a charter school (even one sponsored by the district itself), the state and federal dollars allocated for that child's education move from district to charter. In Dayton, this amounted to serious money. From 2002 to 2005, the dollars flowing to charters grew from about $20 million per annum to almost $45 million. Already stung by the embarrassing loss of students, the district was now starting to feel the fiscal bite from charter competition.

Others, including the state, also noticed what was going on by way of shriveling enrollments in Dayton. Voters had no sooner approved the building levy than the Ohio School Facilities Commission told DPS that it would have to cut the number of new buildings it could construct because of its dwindling pupil numbers. By 2005, Dayton had as large a percentage of its children attending the city's thirty-eight charter schools as any other city in the United States (although post-Katrina New Orleans would soon seize that lead). When word circulated in August of that year that nine organizations had contracts to open even more new charter schools in the city, a backlash ensued.[18]

Reporting on the situation, the *New York Times* observed that Dayton had about as many charter schools as the entire state of New Jersey, "which has a population 50 times larger."[19] Dayton's mayor called for a moratorium on new charters. Littlejohn and Mack held town hall meetings and lobbied political, business, and community leaders to put the brakes on charter schools. The district was disappearing before their eyes and Paul Hill's question three years earlier seemed prophetic. The *Times* reported that "with students leaving to enroll in charters, the city has already had to abandon plans to replace eight schools and more cuts may be required [in the building plan]."[20] Littlejohn lamented that "this once-in-a-lifetime opportunity is slipping through our fingers."[21]

Perhaps so, but like Alaska's infamous bridge to nowhere, what's the point of building schools that have scant likelihood of ever serving students? In fact, the city did build one brand-new school that, when it came time to open, would have few pupils in attendance. But more on that later. Parents and students had been voting with their feet for years and Littlejohn should have been asking why. As house speaker Jon Husted told the *Times*, "The question that the Dayton Public Schools need to ask themselves is, 'Why are all these children leaving?' Instead of blaming charter schools, they should ask, 'What can we do better to make students stay?'"[22]

But even Husted, a devout education free-marketeer, expressed dismay at how quickly charters were growing in his hometown.[23] Editorial writers at the *Dayton Daily News* did, too, writing that "Dayton schools absolutely would not be making some of the reforms they are engaged in if it hadn't been for the pressure that's come from charter schools. The existence of the charters is unquestionably a good thing. But there is such a thing as too much of a good thing."[24] In the summer of 2005, the Ohio General Assembly, led by Husted, capped the state's charter school program, dramatically slowing the growth of new schools in Dayton—and elsewhere.

From 2002 to early 2007, it appeared to most observers, including us, that the district was righting its own boat, however slowly and fitfully. As the *Daily News* observed, charters had forced the district to try to become more customer focused. There were also signs that achievement was ticking upward. Between 1998 and 2004, the Council of the Great City Schools found, the district reduced the reading gap in the early grades (with more mixed results in math).[25] Brightening academic results helped lift DPS out of the Academic Emergency category and into the Continuous Improvement category on the state's all-important report card. DPS was also becoming more efficient.

In 2000, DPS spent only 47 percent of its operating budget on instruction, but by 2004, that figure had risen to 61 percent.[26] The following year, a DPS principal told researchers from Paul Hill's center that "school choice has really put an emphasis on what we do as educators, how we safeguard our schools and our positions. We take a look at how we serve the public, how we service our students, and how we represent the district because of the competition—and it is competition."[27] Another Dayton official stated simply, "It's like you're doing your checkbook. You've got this many bills, and you've got this much money, so you can't get more bills than you have money. It's pretty simple, and I think people understand. If you take another $5,300 away, then you're going to take some people away."[28] It seemed that competition was working. The Dayton public schools were reacting in mostly constructive if still grudging ways.

In February 2007, we surprised many when we wrote in the *Dayton Daily News* that we favored the district's next operating levy request.[29] That op-ed by Terry Ryan summarized where Dayton had been: "It's no secret that my colleagues and I at the Thomas B. Fordham Foundation have been critics of the Dayton Public Schools during the past decade and have done our best—not good enough—to help create sound educational alternatives for kids whose prospects were blighted by the system's failings. We aren't motivated by ill will, much less an animus toward public education. Quite simply, Dayton Public Schools had languished for years as Ohio's lowest performing public school district. . . . And it seemed all but immune to reform."[30] We detailed the gains the district had made over five years and noted that it had improved its efficiency and even made some hard choices regarding job cuts and new spending. We concluded that, for DPS to remain on its reformist course, "the school district now needs help from the city's taxpayers. A 16-mill operating levy will be on the May ballot. The last [operating] levy was passed in 1992. If passed, the operating levy would provide Dayton Public Schools with an additional $30 million per year to continue its reform efforts, raise the quality of instruction and secure the district's finances. If it fails, the district faces a litany of bad choices . . . DPS leadership has been doing its part. Now Daytonians must do theirs."[31]

In the event, the levy did fail and the district did indeed face a Niagara of hard choices, as well as much recrimination and finger pointing. District leaders were now disposed to declare charters a problem, a burden, and a drain of scarce resources. The tension played out in many ways. For example, DPS officials saw the cost of transportation for charter students as unfair. Under Ohio law, districts had long provided the same transportation for parochial school students and had generally done so without complaint. Yet the charter school busing obligation grated on district officials and they could demonstrate that it cost them money (especially as gas prices rose). Superintendent Mack once asked a group of community leaders, "In what other line of business do you have to transport your competitor's customers to their place of business and often on their schedules?"

It did little good to remind Mack and his colleagues that charters are public schools, too, that parents who enroll children in them are taxpayers, too, and that society's obligation is to educate children, not to look after the interests of adults and their institutions. Such theoretical points were usually lost on school system officials faced with declining enrollment and tightening budgets.

By now a weary Gail Littlejohn had stepped down as school board president. (A few months later, she left Ohio for a new job in Houston.) Dr. Mack was rumored to be seeking employment elsewhere. The teachers union was recruiting school board candidates who would help it get out from under the reformist regime. We, and others in Dayton, feared that the brief but welcome period of optimism and rapprochement in the city's education would again be replaced by stasis, envy, and warfare.

Notes

1. Gail Littlejohn, interview by Mike Lafferty, 2008.
2. Editorial, "It's Not Too Soon for Dayton's New City Commission and School Board to Sit Down Together," *Dayton Daily News*, November 8, 2001, 18A.
3. Editorial, "City Schools' Accountability Begins at Top," *Dayton Daily News*, January 1, 2002, 10A.
4. Littlejohn, interview.
5. *Raising Student Achievement*, Council of the Great Cities Report, Dayton, OH, February 2008, 11.
6. Ibid.
7. Ibid.
8. Ibid., 12.
9. Ibid.
10. Scott Elliott, "School District's Bond Issue Plea Pivotal to Many Sectors," *Dayton Daily News*, September 23, 2002, 1A.
11. The *Dayton Daily News* reported the school building venture compared with construction of the Miami Conservancy District in response to the disastrous 1913 Dayton flood. Completed in 1922, that project built five major dams and river levies at a cost of more than $30 million, equivalent to $810 million in 2002.
12. Elliott, "School District's Bond."
13. Terry Ryan, "Dayton Public School Reform," Memorandum to Thomas B. Fordham Foundation Board of Trustees, May 13, 2002.
14. Littlejohn, interview.
15. Catherine Gewertz, "Dayton Feels the Heat from Charter Schools," *Education Week*, April 24, 2002, 1.
16. Littlejohn, interview.
17. Scott Elliott, "District's New Superintendent Welcomes Staff," *Dayton Daily News*, August 22, 2002, 3B.
18. A rumor at the time predicted that as many as twenty-three new schools would be opening, but this was based on faulty information.
19. Sam Dillon, "Charter Schools Alter Map of Education in Dayton," *New York Times*, March 27, 2005, 15.
20. Ibid.
21. Ibid.
22. Ibid.
23. Ibid.
24. Editorial, *Dayton Daily News*, March 13, 2005.
25. Michael Casserly, "Beating the Odds: A City-by-City Analysis of Student Performance and Achievement Gaps on State Assessments," Council of the Great City Schools, http://agi.harvard.edu/Search/download.php?id=53.
26. Scott Elliott, "Pivotal School Year Begins Monday," *Dayton Daily News*, August 23, 2008, 1.

27. Christine Campbell and others, "No Longer the Only Game in Town: Helping Traditional Public Schools Compete," Center on Reinventing Public Education, September 2006, 36.

28. Ibid.

29. The Dayton public schools passed a school facilities levy in 2002, but had not passed an operating levy since 1992.

30. Terry Ryan, "Other Voices: DPS Leaders Have Done Their Part to Turn City Schools Around," *Dayton Daily News*, February 6, 2007.

31. Ibid.

6

Plunging Ahead

By autumn 2003, the dearth of good new charter school sponsors in the Dayton area compelled the Fordham staff to consider recommending—despite misgivings and trepidations—that the foundation itself might have to become an authorizer. In October, we updated our board on the meager yield from the Ohio Charter School Sponsor Institute. Although it had attracted a handful of prospective sponsors, it had not generated any that inspired our confidence. As our memo explained, "Our temptation to have [Fordham] become a charter sponsor arises largely from the fact that, as of this writing, no quality third-party 501(c)3 has thrown its hat into the ring as a potential sponsor for Dayton-area charter schools. After due consideration, however, it is our opinion that we shouldn't add sponsorship to everything else we're trying to do in Dayton, except as a last case scenario. We'd rather offer multiple-levels of support if a quality sponsor emerges in Dayton. If none does, we may yet have to revisit this matter with you on an urgent basis."[1]

There were so many sound reasons for Fordham to eschew sponsorship that a reasonable person could well ask what finally nudged us. Legal liabilities were serious concerns. There was the risk to Fordham's reputation as well as the foundation's lack of relevant real-world experience. Another question was whether a sponsorship agreement that met all of Fordham's concerns could be negotiated with the Ohio Department of Education.

Would this resolutely private organization be turned into a quasi-public agency, and if so with what loss of confidentiality and nimbleness? Would our staff be overwhelmed by bureaucratic minutiae and compliance headaches? And how much would sponsorship actually cost? At the time, the foundation's endowment totaled $41 million, which provided a little more than $2 million a year to cover our costs and grants, both in Ohio and nationally. Fordham could likely handle the direct expense of sponsorship itself, but how much would be left for everything else that we did and wanted to keep doing?

Due Diligence

We fretted, too, about the risks that sponsorship would pose to our endowment and possibly to board members and their families. But after extensive discussions with outside experts and some pricey legal research we understood that those risks could be mitigated through well-crafted charter school contracts, thoughtful operational policies and procedures—and plenty of insurance. This conclusion was summed up in another board memo: "In short, a carefully crafted Directors and Officers policy, combined with an Errors and Omissions policy, and perhaps, an Employment Practices and Liability policy, will insure both the Fordham Foundation and its trustees (and their spouses) against the full gamut of potential lawsuits."[2]

The legal hazards were at least informed by law and precedent but other challenges proved more perplexing. The risk to Fordham's reputation was hard to gauge. Could a team of practiced, even proficient policy wonks actually run an on-the-ground sponsorship operation? Board chairman David Ponitz remembers the discussions, which stretched over several meetings. Although the retired Sinclair Community College president and longtime community leader personally felt that Fordham needed to become a sponsor, he tried to help the board reach a consensus. "The board understands there will be differences of opinion," Ponitz said in a 2008 interview:

> The group listens to one another really well and respects one another. . . .
> There was always debate [but] . . . the issue changed from [being] muddled to "I'm not sure how this vote will come out," to people raising a lot of questions but being careful as to how they might come down on the issue if there was a vote, to understanding this is what we should do. . . . Is it right? Will it help children learn? What can we learn from it? What are the pitfalls? How many of those can be eliminated? Money? . . . It was more of a Japanese-style of decision making . . . working through all the issues, then deciding, then to get going. . . . [But] all the way through Diane Ravitch opposed it. I was never sure of the decision until the end.[3]

Ravitch, a respected and high-profile education historian, as well as Finn's longtime friend and collaborator, objected to the cost, the time, and the effort for something that was distant from the customary work of a policy research organization. She told an *Education Week* reporter, "I don't think think-tanks should run schools, but I was outvoted." She continued, "Checker is a controversial figure and I told him he would have a target on his back."[4] Other board members shared her concern about whether Fordham could effectively staff and manage a sponsorship operation. This was very different from conducting studies, issuing reports, and offering opinions.

Yet most board members were at least open to the idea—provided that their questions were answered reasonably. "I thought we should do it because this would give us a more hands-on approach to doing what we said we wanted to do, which was to create quality charter schools in Dayton," said Bruno Manno in an interview for this book. Manno is Senior Advisor to the Foundation's K–12 Education Reform Initiative at the Walton Family Foundation and is one of the nation's leading experts on charter schools and authorizing. "You can only do so much as a foundation. Being an authorizer puts you in a different position," he believes.[5]

Education Week captured this challenge as well when it reported that "the Fordham Foundation appears to be the only think tank in the country to serve as a charter school authorizer. . . . Fordham's move into charter authorizing comes amid concern about the poor academic performance of many Ohio charters and as advocates nationally are calling for greater attention to the role authorizers play in charter quality. Fordham officials say they hope the foundation will be a model authorizer, even while acknowledging that the proposition is a risk that could ultimately tarnish the organization's reputation."[6] Despite concerns, there was an upside, and one not to be taken lightly. As Manno noted, we stood to learn a great deal from sponsorship. For example, how much influence could a sponsor, largely motivated by making a difference in the lives of children, actually have on the academic and financial performance of its schools? Here was a chance not only to encourage, kibitz, and criticize other sponsors but also to use what the foundation took away from the experience to improve how sponsors work, both in Ohio and beyond.

As staff explained to the board, "The idea of a nationally known foundation, with a non-trivial history of involvement in Dayton and national education reform issues, actually sponsoring charter schools is an exciting notion that would be studied, and scrutinized, by others across the United States. That's the risk and reward in a nutshell This is an opportunity for us not only to generate ideas, but also to put them into practice."[7]

While Fordham had no direct experience in the sponsor's role, our team wasn't ignorant about it. In June 2003 we published *Charter School Authorizing: Are States Making the Grade?*, a study that drew us deep into identifying what worked and what didn't in the sponsorship realm. It also noted the central challenge facing authorizers across the country: holding schools to account for real and measurable academic achievement without overwhelming them with red tape and meddling. Through survey data from 24 states with 509 authorizers, it provided examples of cities (e.g., Chicago) and states (such as Massachusetts) where authorizing was done well, as well as places where it was not, including the Ohio Department of Education. It probed authorizer policies and practices that worked and those that didn't. The Fordham board also contained serious charter school expertise, which included Manno and Finn, who in 2000 had coauthored, with former foundation vice president Gregg Vanourek, *Charter Schools in Action*. On the ground in Dayton, Fordham had worked closely with charter schools since the first one opened in 1998, supporting them by means of direct grants, a resource center that we helped to birth, and a statewide advocacy group. We had also made some blunders. In hindsight, we gave start-up grants to charter operators in Dayton who should never have opened schools. Some of these schools—City Day, the Rhea Academy, and the Colin Powell Leadership Academy—would produce such abysmal results as to give a black eye to the charter concept in Dayton and statewide.

The founder of City Day was convicted of crimes related to school operations, while the Rhea Academy closed under a cloud of fiscal scandal. The Colin Powell Leadership Academy would ultimately close under pressure of a lawsuit from the Ohio Attorney General. Innocently we had supposed at the outset that any school with the word "charter" in its name deserved a helping hand.

To help troubled schools while also germinating strong new ones, we worked for several years with the Dayton Area Chamber of Commerce and local philanthropists to support an Education Resource Center (ERC). It provided an array of services to start-up charter schools. We invested hundreds of thousands of dollars in grants to ERC, as well as direct start-up help for individual schools. One could fairly say we tried in every way we could to help create a charter sector from scratch in a community whose children deserved educational alternatives. There was no recipe for how to do this at all, let alone how to do it well.

The ERC's assistance to schools included help with writing grants, developing business plans, creating and refining academic programs and curricula, and testing, as well as such back-office operations as accounting. It tried whenever possible to persuade schools to share services. These were small organizations, after all, and could extract economies of scale and perhaps greater quality if a critical mass could be assembled to acquire an important service. For example, the ERC organized a pretesting and posttesting program across multiple schools to gauge how much charter pupils gained over the course of a school year.

Our encouragement of this inevitably led to the question, "How can test results be seen as credible if an avowed supporter of school choice coordinates them?" But someone needed to determine whether these new schools were adding value to their students. We knew their state test scores would be weak—at least for the first few years—because the youngsters entering them came from woefully performing district schools in which they clearly had not thrived. But the charters should still be adding value, and that could be measured.[8]

Through writings, talks, seminars, testimony, and conference participation, we also strove to share as widely as we could the lessons we were learning by working with charter school operators in various capacities. (This book is in part a culmination of that analysis-and-dissemination effort.)

Yet for all of this prolonged and diverse experience with charter schools in Ohio and beyond, we still weren't sure we had what it took to build a competent sponsorship operation. It is one thing to help organizations helping schools, to offer grants to schools, to study schools, and to write about them ourselves. It is very different to be legally responsible for real schools attended by real children. Eventually, Fordham took the plunge. Eight days in advance of its 2004 winter board meeting, Finn sent members a page-and-a-half memo. Looming in June 2005 was the end of the state's two-year grace period for "orphaned" schools to find new sponsors, and Finn gave his thoughts with customary directness.

Yet his note illustrates how conflicted we were. At the same time, he wrote, there was a decent opportunity to succeed at something that few, perhaps no other think tank had ever done—to come down from the mountain top and get its hands dirty in the real world. Dayton was at an education crossroads and Fordham needed to examine itself and its work there, to peer inward and ask exactly how well it was doing its job:

> Can we do [sponsorship] well? No guarantees. But we have a fighting chance. With your help, and a lot of hard work, it's more than possible. True, we'll be in the spotlight. True, we could stumble. But I believe everyone will respect us for trying, for taking the chance that I am convinced we must take. Indeed if we don't, I believe we should pull way back on our Dayton program and concentrate on the national stuff where we *know* we can add value. Moreover, if we don't do this, there's no good reason for us to continue to have an on-the-ground presence in Dayton and I would expect [Vice President for Ohio Programs and Policy] Terry [Ryan] to move his family back to Washington when convenient for them.[9]

The board vote to proceed with sponsorship was seven in favor and one abstention—by Diane Ravitch.

Sponsorship Agreement Negotiation

The Fordham staff entered into contract negotiations with the Ohio Department of Education (ODE) even before the board voted. Ours was the first nonprofit organization to go through the state's new authorizer application process. We had to convince the State Board of Education and leaders at ODE that we would be a fit sponsor. We had to show state bureaucrats what roles we would and wouldn't play in school operations, the kinds of technical assistance we would provide, and how we would monitor schools, assess progress, and intervene when one started to run off the rails.

Monitoring, for example, would involve reporting and analyzing data provided by schools as well as on-site inspections. We were required to ensure that schools complied with applicable laws and regulations but we did not want to get in the way of the people actually running them. We shared our theory of sponsorship with *Education Week*: "If [schools] are organizationally strong and they're delivering the goods, our approach is to, as much as possible, stay out of their way and encourage their development and improvement."[10] We believed in letting people do their jobs but also in conscientiously monitoring them. "Everybody benefits from having somebody watching over their shoulder," Finn said.

The state's hot-off-the-presses sponsorship application posed eleven questions, including: How would we provide technical assistance? What is our philosophy for assessing student progress and monitoring the school's academic performance? How would Fordham ensure that its schools didn't break the law? How would we intervene to correct problems? What are the elements of a good school? ODE wanted answers to these queries and many more. We understood that our answers would be graded by the same agency that not so long before had been given a failing mark for its own sponsorship work by the state auditor and the general assembly. Still, our answers ran to thirteen single-spaced pages.

We stated, for the first of what would be many times, that we do "not believe it is appropriate for a sponsor to also be the vendor of additional fee-based services, so we are keeping the role of sponsor separate from that of supplemental service provider."[11] This was a critical point because we saw it as an inherent conflict of interest when a sponsor also functioned— as many in Ohio did—as the (paid) purveyor of services to its schools. It was the sponsor's role, we believed, to point schools in need of fiscal, special education, and other services toward competent providers, but to play no role in a school's decisions about which services to procure from which vendors.

In our view, these blurring of responsibilities and services inevitably clouded the oversight issue, particularly a sponsor's duty to close a non-functioning school. Shuttering a school is hard enough, but closing a charter school that is providing multiple streams of revenue to its sponsor is akin to killing a goose that is laying golden eggs for its owner. And, the bigger the school the bigger the goose and its golden eggs.

Our sponsorship application also set forth an approach to intervening
in troubled schools:

> Our theory of intervention rests on the following precepts: (a) ounce of
> prevention; if we know enough about a school early enough we can help it
> nip problems in the bud by pointing them out and requesting or demand-
> ing that the school address them; (b) making everything transparent in the
> school contract; including "what happens if "; (c) doing our best to encour-
> age schools to solve problems through a variety of notices, threats, and
> limited interventions such as putting a school on probation, plus referral
> to sources of technical assistance. We're not averse to closing a school but
> would rather help one get fixed.[12]

On March 8, 2004, we submitted our application to ODE and began to
negotiate the details of a sponsorship agreement. Most of it was fairly well
defined by statute. For example, Fordham's term of agreement was seven
years commencing July 1, 2004. We agreed to enter into contracts with no
more than thirty schools. Sponsor duties and responsibilities were spelled
out, along with stipulations regarding "revocation of sponsorship authority" and the right to appeal. It was clear that Fordham could charge a sponsorship fee of up to 3 percent of the total state funding that a charter school
received. What wasn't clear was what the statute actually meant when it said
that sponsors will "monitor and evaluate the community school's compliance at least annually with *all* laws and rules applicable to the school."

We argued that responsibility for compliance monitoring of every
applicable state and federal law would be prohibitive for nongovernmental
sponsors and was probably not the legislature's intent. Special education
was particularly important because it was so heavily regulated and was
already overseen by ODE's Office of Exceptional Children. What was the
division of labor between sponsors and that office?

The federal Individuals with Disabilities Education Act (IDEA) made
clear that the state is ultimately responsible for ensuring a free and appropriate public education for such children and may delegate responsibility for implementation to school districts and, in Ohio, to charter school
governing authorities. Nowhere does IDEA even contemplate any delega-
tion of state responsibility for special education to a private entity outside
this framework, such as a nonprofit charter sponsor. We sought written
guidance from ODE, but they were hesitant to provide guidance that went
beyond the vague definitions of state law.

There was also uncertainty around "technical assistance." Ohio's charter
statute tasked sponsors with providing schools relevant knowledge, expertise, and resources, including, but not limited to, training, information,

written materials, and manuals.[13] The same statute also tasked ODE itself with providing technical assistance to sponsors and schools.[14] So the division of labor between state and sponsor was murky. We worried that this ambiguity could easily lead to space for a lawsuit, or turn out to be an area where anticharter lawmakers or bureaucrats could criticize Fordham.

To address such uncertainties, our attorneys proposed an "addendum to sponsorship agreement" that spelled out ODE's acknowledgments and responsibilities. In it, the state agency would agree, among other items, to "timely notify the Sponsor, either through its training sessions or by written notice, of additions, modifications and changes in the community schools' laws, regulations and rules." The department also defined the laws and rules for which a sponsor is required to monitor compliance.[15]

In this way, we sought to erect a fence around what we were actually responsible for doing as a sponsor. With this addendum agreed to, the sponsorship contract between Fordham and the state was signed on September 8, 2004. We were now in a position to take on charter schools as an official sponsor, beginning July 1, 2005. And state school chieftain Susan T. Zelman was now in a position to tease Finn that she had become, in one key role anyway, his supervisor.

Devilish Economics

The charter school marketplace in Ohio was sorely unsettled, making it difficult to estimate what sponsorship would actually cost to do well. In February 2004, it looked as if as many as twenty-two orphaned Dayton charters would need to find alternate sponsors or be forced to close. Not all of these schools deserved to be sponsored, but some certainly did. A few months later, even as Fordham was filing its application to become an authorizer, we learned that our worry about orphaned schools was exaggerated. As noted earlier, the Lucas County Education Service Center (LCESC) was seeking to build a statewide charter school sponsorship empire and was offering cheap and hassle-free sponsorship to schools all over Ohio.[16]

Nonprofit organizations such as the Buckeye Community Hope Foundation in Cincinnati and Kids Count Ohio in Dayton, as well as other county education service centers, were also stepping into sponsorship. Furthermore, although the University of Toledo had ceased direct authorizing in 2001, it had spun off its sponsorship operation into the independent Ohio Council of Community Schools. Led by the energetic daughter of former legislator Sally Perz, the council soon came to rival LCESC as the state's largest and most enterprising charter empire builder.

Few of these willing sponsors seemed to be sticklers for academic achievement. They made little mention of results-based accountability or pupil learning in their marketing materials. In contrast, everyone knew that Fordham was dead serious about the essential charter school bargain of operational freedoms in return for results. We spelled out our theory of sponsorship for all to see:

> Schools should be as free as possible from bureaucratic red-tape, external micro-management and indiscriminate demands, so they can focus on educating children and young adults. However, freedom comes with the responsibility to produce results (accountability) and to provide information to those who seek it (transparency). A quality sponsor should work with its schools to create contracts that accurately set forth what the schools will do, how they will do it, and how their results will be appraised. The sponsor then holds the school to the terms of its contract. If the school does what it promised, it deserves to be supported and sustained. If not, the sponsor's job is to push it to improve while providing it with access to top-quality technical assistance. If over time the school cannot or will not deliver the promised results, it has no right to continue.[17]

Although not bottomless, Fordham's pockets were deep enough that we could operate as a sponsor without great risk of going broke. Nevertheless, the economics of sponsorship were much discussed at our February and June 2004 board meetings. At the first of those, staff presented an estimate of $190,000 in sponsorship start-up costs, but by June that projection had more than doubled. Skyrocketing legal fees associated with limiting Fordham's potential liability were the main reason. These costs would never be recouped and would come out of Fordham's endowment, especially considering that school fees would not start flowing until July 2005.

Ongoing costs and revenues were even harder to estimate. It was difficult to nail down reasonable assumptions for such crucial variables as how many schools we would ultimately sponsor over a period of years; how many children they might enroll; how many schools might close midcontract; and the fees that these schools would pay. Expense assumptions were not much more robust. For example, if a school had to be closed against its will, legal costs could spike. Acknowledging much uncertainty, we assumed for purposes of budget projections that we would sponsor eight schools at the start of the 2005 to 2006 year and that these would collectively yield about $300,000 annually in fees. (We estimated that they would educate 3,200 children and pay an average 1.5 percent sponsorship fee, equivalent to about $90 a child.)

Costs were estimated to run about $391,000 a year and would grow from there. As school fees would not cover Fordham's expenses, we were looking at subsidizing the sponsorship operation to the tune of some $100,000 a year for the first three years. Our optimistic longer-term scenario called for school fees to match sponsorship costs by 2008. The worst-case scenario was indeed a fiscal black hole—a subsidy of at least $1.4 million between June 2004 and July 2008, with more to follow.

Big-Time Help

Troubled by these uncertainties and potential costs, Fordham sought help from others with deeper pockets. In late 2004, Finn spoke with senior education staff at the megabucks Bill and Melinda Gates Foundation. They were receptive and, on May 11, 2005, Fordham submitted to Gates a proposal to fund "Sponsorship Infrastructure Development and Support." It contemplated a significant expansion of the Fordham sponsorship operation. We sought $1.8 million over three years (2005 to 2008) to do the following:

1. Become the high-quality statewide sponsor of charter schools in Ohio
2. Recruit proven, high-quality school developers and operators to open schools in the state, particularly high schools, and sponsor those schools
3. Contribute to the development of best practices in charter authorizing, viewing that as a possible model for the future governance of public education itself
4. Become a model of quality sponsorship from which school districts and other not-for-profit organizations, in Ohio and beyond, can learn

We told Gates that its money would enable us to widen sponsorship from Dayton to Cincinnati and Columbus, and ultimately statewide. By 2008, we figured, we could have thirty schools serving upward of eight thousand students. The additional dollars, we believed, would also enable us to be on the cutting edge of sponsorship nationally. For example, we proposed to help develop an Authorizer Oversight Information System for Ohio to automate many of the paper-based compliance functions of a sponsor. We intended to offer "performance reward sponsorship," that is, reduced-cost sponsorship, even free sponsorship, for academically high-performing schools. We wanted to provide high-quality board training to Fordham-sponsored schools as well as other interested schools and sponsors across

Ohio. And we would prepare an annual report that would include a self-appraisal of our own performance as an authorizer as well as the academic performance of all Fordham-sponsored schools.

We were ambitious, hopeful, and full of beans. We even proposed to assist, free of charge, school districts that were game to sponsor bona fide charter schools.

In January 2005, we wrote an op-ed in the *Columbus Dispatch* that urged district officials in places like Dayton and Columbus to seriously consider a "tight-loose" portfolio of schools akin to Fordham's charter-sponsor relationship. Such a structure would empower individual schools to manage themselves and still be accountable for academic performance. Superintendents could act less like bureaucratic overseers and more like direction setters. "This is a very big deal," we wrote, "nothing less than the restructuring of public education from bureaucratic dinosaur to modern organization. . . . Ohio school districts have an opportunity to use charter schools as assets, and such efforts deserve strong support."[18]

After much back and forth, in September 2005 Gates proffered a $1.85 million grant to be paid out over three years. Now we felt equipped to tackle the opportunities and challenges to come. But even with this support we sensed the presence of trolls under the sponsorship bridge. In the final proposal to Gates, we observed that "the largest external risk to the success of the project outlined above is possible adverse changes in state laws pertaining to sponsorship and charter schools generally. (Court decisions could have the same effect.) This proposal is contingent on state law continuing to enable Fordham to sponsor in a manner that does not impose unacceptable financial and legal risks upon our board of trustees or staff members. A secondary risk is senior personnel changes within the Ohio Department of Education that result in the hiring of staff that are less enthusiastic about charter schools."[19] On July 1, 2005, Fordham assumed responsibility for ten extant charter schools. They collectively served about three thousand children and employed two hundred teachers in Cincinnati, Dayton, and Springfield. While most served K through 8 students, a few served some pupils in the high school grades. Their enrollments were significantly more African American than the districts in which they were located (91 vs. 63 percent). (White students made up 73 percent of Ohio's total public school population.)

Students in Fordham-sponsored schools were also poorer, with nearly 85 percent of them participating in the federal Free and Reduced Lunch program versus 62 percent of pupils in the three urban districts where the schools were located. (Statewide, 35 percent of public school students qualified for the lunch subsidy.) These schools, we knew, were operating with about 30 percent less per-pupil funding than local district schools,[20] and doing so in a hostile political environment where districts across the state reflexively blamed charters for their worsening fiscal pain. "It's alarming," said Groveport-Madison Superintendent Timm Mackley in 2005. "All of us superintendents in Franklin County [Columbus area] anticipated there might be a ceiling somewhere where the people interested in alternative choices would be exhausted. If there's a ceiling, we haven't hit it yet."[21]

First Setback

Even as we prepared to launch our sponsorship efforts, Ohio legislators put a serious crimp in our plans. House Bill 66, proposed in February 2005 and signed into law in June 2005, was actually sponsored by procharter Republicans and is best seen as a political reaction to the rapid and irresponsible empire building of the Lucas County Education Service Center. That body's reckless opportunism resulted in many ill-prepared school operators opening schools almost overnight in Ohio's big cities.

In Dayton, it triggered a political uproar, which became apparent to the whole country in spring 2005 when the *New York Times* published a story on the explosive growth of charter schools there. Lucas County had visions of sponsoring 180 charter schools by 2006, fifty more than were run by the state's largest district. The *Columbus Dispatch* reported in July 2005, just after passage of the bill capping Lucas County and the entire charter program, that lawmakers were skeptical of the number of new schools hoping to open. The second-ranking state senator at the time, Dayton's Jeff Jacobson, told the newspaper, "The numbers involved just did not pass the smell test."[22]

In response, House Bill 66 imposed a statewide cap that limited the charter sector to thirty new schools. This abrupt lid placing led to a strange and contentious moment, because some sixty-two new schools were already planning to open the very next month—and had been granted charters by various authorizers. They now had to participate in a hasty lottery by which the thirty available slots would be allotted. The legislature gave ODE thirty days to conduct such a lottery. As the *Dispatch* reported, "by the spin of the bingo wheel" prospective school operators learned whether or not they were actually going to be able to open their schools.[23]

The bill did more than place a cap on school numbers. It also sought once more to put some oomph into charter standards and accountability. Senator Joy Padgett, who chaired the education committee at the time, told *Education Week* that the law would help make Ohio "a leader in accountability for e-schools and charter schools. Ohio, I believe, definitely is a story of choice [in education]," she said. "Fine, we're just going to make sure those choices have standards."[24] The new statute also imposed a death penalty on persistently failing charter schools. The existence of too many such schools was an affront to lawmakers who had supported the charter concept. Henceforth, schools that didn't help students improve on state reading and math tests over a three-year period faced automatic closure.

In addition to the statewide cap on new schools, the law placed limits on individual sponsors. Lucas County was restricted to seventy-five schools and other sponsors to fifty apiece. (As Fordham's cap was already contractually set at thirty schools, this provision had no direct effect on our efforts, although the statewide ceiling meant we would have difficulty opening new schools.) There was also a moratorium placed on new e-schools, making it impossible for more cybercharters to open. That one would really limit our ability to entice quality virtual-school operators to the Buckeye State.

The law did, however, create an "operator exemption" for high-performing charter schools. This meant that a governing board could open a new school outside the cap so long as it did so in partnership with a school operator that was already running an academically successful charter school elsewhere. Thus, an organization that was running at least one high-performing charter (in Ohio or another state) had the leeway to open another school in Ohio. In practice, this came to mean that the only entities that could launch new schools in the Buckeye State were proven nonprofit or for-profit charter management organizations. The days of someone with big ideas and high hopes but no track record opening an Ohio charter school were over.

We supported those elements of House Bill 66 that sought to solve Ohio's charter-quality problem. As Finn told the *Columbus Dispatch* in the midst of debate around the bill, "There are some wonderful [charter] schools where kids are learning tons. But there are a bunch ticking along in Academic Emergency or Academic Watch with nobody seeming to care much. I think that's a damn shame."[25] Speaker Jon Husted cared, however, and said as much to *Education Week*: "We have a number of [charter] schools that are successful. We think they will be able to hit these marks quite easily." As for chronic low performers, he said, "Either get the job done or get out."[26]

Besides its many charter-related elements, House Bill 66 put further competitive pressure on existing schools—district and charter alike—by creating a statewide voucher program. Dubbed the Ohio Education Choice Scholarship, up to fourteen thousand students attending persistently failing public schools would be allowed to attend private schools of their choice. The vouchers provided up to $4,250 for students in grades K through 8 and $5,000 for high school students.

This measure represented an earnest attempt by lawmakers to revamp education in troubled districts and create new quality education opportunities for children, while repairing the state's troubled charter program. In an op-ed, Ryan observed, it would "boost accountability for charter schools, while keeping them as options for children and assuring that they continue to put needed pressure on low-performing school systems."[27] But we also noted that the bill compounded some problems—in particular, the following:

- Charters would remain underfunded and still got no help with facilities.

- Virtual charter schools faced a host of new rules and funding limits that would likely harm the good ones in the name of deterring bad ones.

- A statewide cap remained on the total number of charters that could open, obviously constraining everyone's capacity to launch solid new ones.

- Little was done to encourage districts to embrace the charter option as part of their overall reform strategies.[28]

The *Columbus Dispatch* got it about right when it editorialized that "the charter school idea should be simple: Private entities willing to try new ideas in education are given public funds and freed from many rules, in exchange for a promise to deliver certain results. If the legislature will make necessary changes to hold them accountable for those promises, charter schools can play an important role in improving education for all Ohio children."[29] The changes wrought by House Bill 66 were mostly good but came at a bad time for our nascent sponsorship efforts. We would come to discover that it now took Herculean efforts to open high-quality schools in Ohio—and that fixing broken schools would be even more difficult.

Notes

1. "Ohio Charter School Sponsor Institute," Memorandum to Thomas B. Fordham Foundation Board of Trustees, October 21, 2003.
2. "Questions and Answers about Charter-School Sponsorship," Memorandum to Thomas B. Fordham Foundation Board of Trustees, February 3, 2004.
3. David Ponitz, interview by Mike Lafferty, July 8, 2008.
4. Erik W. Robelen, "A Think Tank Takes the Plunge," *Education Week*, December 20, 2006.
5. Bruno Manno, interview by Mike Lafferty, July 14, 2008.
6. Robelen, "A Think Tank."

7. "Questions and Answers."

8. In 2007, Ohio implemented its own "value-added" accountability component, which reports, school by school, on how much pupils advanced academically during the previous year in comparison with how much they were "expected" to gain.

9. Chester E. Finn, Jr., Thomas B. Fordham Internal Board Memorandum, February 3, 2004.

10. Robelen, "A Think Tank."

11. Thomas B. Fordham Foundation, "Community School Sponsorship Application," Ohio Department of Education, March 8, 2004.

12. Ibid.

13. Ohio Administrative Code 3301-102-02(U).

14. Ohio Revised Code 3314.015(A).

15. Sponsorship Agreement authorizing the Thomas B. Fordham Foundation as a community school sponsor, September 8, 2004.

16. State law required "the sponsor of a community [charter] school to be located or have representatives located within fifty miles of the location of the community school," but this provision was liberally interpreted by ODE.

17. Thomas B. Fordham Foundation, "Should the Fordham Foundation Sponsor Your Charter School?" March 5, 2004.

18. Terry Ryan, "Public Schools Seeing Worth of Charter-School Venues," *Columbus Dispatch*, January 28, 2005.

19. Grant proposal to the Bill and Melinda Gates Foundation from the Thomas B. Fordham Foundation, May 11, 2005.

20. Sheree Speakman and others, *Charter School Funding: Inequity's Next Frontier*, Thomas B. Fordham Institute, Dayton, OH, August 2005, 106.

21. Jennifer Smith Richards, "Suburbs Feel Charters' Pinch—School Leaders outside City Try to Stem Loss of Students to Urban Alternatives," *Columbus Dispatch*, October 23, 2005, 1B.

22. Jennifer Smith Richards, "New Limits on Charter Schools Hit Some Hard," *Columbus Dispatch*, July 7, 2005, 1A.

23. Charlie Roduta, "Seven New Charter Schools Seek Students, Staff, Buildings—Stricter State Rules, Discerning Parents Intensify the Battle in the Marketplace," *Columbus Dispatch*, August 16, 2005, 5D.

24. Erik W. Robelen, "Ohio Mandates New Tests for Charters," *Education Week*, July 27, 2005.

25. Jennifer Smith Richards, "Heat Turned Up on Charters—Budget Takes Aim at Subpar Schools, Expands Vouchers," *Columbus Dispatch*, June 23, 2005, 1A.

26. Robelen, "Ohio Mandates."

27. Terry Ryan, "Chance Is at Hand to Improve Charter Schools," *Columbus Dispatch*, June 11, 2005, A10.

28. Ibid.

29. Editorial, "Proceed with Caution—State Should Allow New Charter Schools Only if Performance Guarantees Are in Place," *Columbus Dispatch*, April 12, 2005, 8A.

7

Baptism Under Fire

Since the state had capped new charters, in Fordham's new role as sponsor we decided to focus our energy, leverage, and money—as well as that of the Gates Foundation—on helping our initial ten schools to improve. They were a varied bunch. Eight had previously been sponsored by the Ohio Department of Education, schools that the department had been required by House Bill 364 to cut loose. The other two were allowed to open by virtue of winning tickets in the 2005 charter school lottery. Both were sister schools of Cincinnati's acclaimed W. E. B. DuBois Academy and were to be run by the DuBois leadership.

We knew from our initial vetting that most preexisting schools faced problems of one sort of another and assumed that we could work with them to boost their performance. Their challenges generally paralleled those of charter schools across Ohio. Among the eight, one was rated Excellent by the state in 2005 (DuBois) and one was rated Continuous Improvement (Dayton Academy, an Edison-operated school), but the remaining six were in Academic Emergency. (At the time, 60 percent of Ohio's charter schools were rated in Academic Emergency, 11 percent in Academic Watch, 18 percent in Continuous Improvement, and just 11 percent Effective or Excellent.[1])

Troubled Schools

When we signed sponsorship agreements with these schools, we knew that several were in serious trouble. In one case, we limited our initial commitment to a thirteen-month contract. (With the others, our contracts ran for five years.) The Moraine Community School had struggled since opening in 2002. But surely it was worth trying to rehabilitate. It represented this Dayton suburb's only public school. Moraine was a General Motors industrial town and many of its families were connected to the GM plant that had once made Frigidaires and now built sport utility vehicles. (The last vehicle, however, rolled off its assembly line on December 23, 2008. The sprawling factory is now dark.)

Before the charter opened, all Moraine students were bused to schools in the nearby suburbs of Kettering and West Carrolton. Many felt like strangers there and they and their parents longed for a neighborhood school of their own. For that reason, the Moraine charter originally enjoyed the support of community leaders and served about two hundred children in grades K through 12. Nevertheless, it encountered serious governance, leadership, financial, and academic difficulties almost from the start. The school was in Academic Emergency for two years prior to Fordham sponsorship and its board and principal went through a nasty split just before we took over. There was a serious leadership vacuum. Our sponsorship agreement made clear that we expected it to improve markedly—and fast. And its board assented. According to our contract, the school would show the following:

- Adequate academic gains from autumn 2005 to spring 2006, as measured on a nationally norm referenced test
- Market demand for the school by enrolling at least 225 students by April 2006
- Compliance with all special education requirements by October 2005
- Implementation of a viable curriculum by February 2006

The school made progress in special-education compliance, in part because we also gave them grant support to purchase outside expertise. But as the February deadline approached we received a letter from the school's board president stating that "our one year sponsorship agreement had renewal terms that we likely won't meet. There was an opportunity to secure 2006/2007 sponsorship through the Cincinnati-based ERCO (Education Resources Consultants)."

With those words, Fordham learned, the Moraine school was fleeing our tough-love embrace. We had thought its leaders were game to make the hard decisions needed to render their school effective. We were wrong, and they spurned us for a less demanding sponsor. What's more, under Ohio law the school was within its legal rights to "sponsor hop" when its leadership team realized we were serious about holding them to account for improving their school.

In 2007, the Moraine school and three others (with no Fordham sponsorship connections) would be sued by Ohio Attorney General Marc Dann. Citing a failure to educate children, Dann asked the Montgomery County Common Pleas Court to declare the school a failed "charitable trust" and enjoin its governing body from operating a charter school. In ruling against the attorney general on legal grounds, the judge concurred in the academic diagnosis: "There is no question," he wrote, "that MCS [Moraine Community School] has performed dismally for the entire period of its existence. For that reason, the Court agrees with the Ohio Attorney General that the State ought to be able to take action with respect to closing the school. As set forth below, however, this Court cannot permit MCS to be closed under the trust laws of the State of Ohio because MCS is not a charitable trust."[2] The Moraine school had certainly brought this criticism upon itself and the judge's appraisal of the situation was spot-on.[3] So was the attorney general's.

In hindsight, we were deluded about the Moraine school and our ability through tough love to turn it around. No matter how much we wanted it to succeed academically, those in charge of it simply did not have the capacity—the school leadership and teachers—to make it perform at a high level. Even more important, based on the numerous conversations we had with the school's board leadership, it was clear to us that they simply did not see their primary mission as delivering academic success to children.

For them, the goal was to provide a place that cared for the community's children with love, respect, and understanding. If learning also occurred, well and good, but the school's very existence was a sufficient end in itself for the board and many parents. It was, quite simply, "their" school. Our efforts to inject a sense of urgency and focus on academic results did not fly with them. That we didn't share the same values should have been obvious from the start. But we failed to see it.

Technical Assistance

As a sponsor, we did not just use threats and deadlines to effect improvements. As the Moraine episode shows, threats could easily be sloughed off by schools that wanted to avoid accountability or simply didn't care. Within the bounds of state law and our budget, we also provided technical assistance to "our" sponsored schools to improve their performance. For example, we offered all those in Academic Emergency expert counsel on how to use achievement data to improve instruction, develop a strategy for maximizing performance on state assessments, and help students gain test-taking prowess.

For that, we engaged nationally known expert Douglas Reeves and his team at the Denver-based Center for Performance Assessment (CPA). Participating schools were provided in November 2005 with the tools to analyze their own test data to ascertain where their students needed the most help. In February 2006, CPA trainers conducted sessions at each

we could charge schools sponsorship fees of up to 3 percent of their per-pupil funding, but our schools were paying closer to 1 percent and several received free sponsorship[6]As a result, over the first four years of our sponsorship work, school fees covered just 30 percent of costs.

Even as we provided the schools with financial and technical assistance at considerable cost to our own budget and with help from the Gates Foundation, we continued to remind ourselves, the schools, and the state that we would not cross the line into providing direct services nor would we charge schools anything beyond their sponsorship fees. In June 2006, we shared a formal policy along those lines with every Fordham-sponsored school, building on what we had told the Ohio Department of Education in our sponsorship application two years earlier. In short, our provision of technical assistance was a good-faith effort to help schools improve, but, at the end of the day, they were responsible for their results and we were responsible for holding them to account for those results.

Our refusal to sell services to sponsored schools proved prescient in the long run, as became obvious when a Columbus charter blew up in 2007. Its collapse resulted in much finger-pointing between sponsor and school as to who was responsible—and liable—for what. The Harte Crossroads School was opened in a mall across from the statehouse, and its birth—and subsequent demise—was well chronicled by the *Columbus Dispatch* in a series of front-page stories. The woman running the school had been vice president of the Ohio Charter School Association and was well known in the charter community nationally. We had worked with her on several earlier projects. Within three years of opening, the school closed abruptly due to terminal financial maladies. Anita Nelam and her board blamed the sponsor (Richland Academy for the Arts) and its management affiliate (the for-profit Innovative Learning Solutions [ILS]) for the school's fiscal woes.

The sponsor and ILS pointed fingers back at Nelam. In a three-page letter to the Ohio Department of Education, her attorney claimed that "after Harte terminated Richland's (ILS) consulting agreement on Dec. 5, 2006, Richland (the sponsor) continued to help itself to 20 percent of the school's foundation payment for the months of December, January and February, totaling in excess of $100,000."[7] Richland countered that "things have been dire for a long time there. They go back to the first year of operation. The financial woes were there."[8] State officials responded to this blizzard of charges and countercharges by stating bluntly that "the state will go after anyone who handled money for the schools to find out who is responsible. That includes founder Anita Nelam; the treasurer, the previous sponsor; and Innovative Learning Solutions."[9]

As of the writing of this book, the state was still trying to sort out these tangles. In any case, this cautionary tale strengthened our conviction that sponsors ought not ever sell supplemental services to their schools. Unfortunately, many sponsors in Ohio made—and today still make—their own ends meet by doing precisely that. That's why legislation introduced in 2006 and 2007 to prohibit sponsors from selling supplemental services to their schools failed to become law. It would have unbalanced the books of too many sponsors. But neither did lawmakers solve the underlying problems of sponsor funding in Ohio: the chronic need to raise operating funds from the schools themselves, whether by charging fees or selling services, combined with the perverse incentives and inherent role conflicts that arise when saying no to a school, is tantamount to reducing one's own revenue.

Dollars and Cents

Sponsors weren't the only ones on the Ohio charter scene to face financial challenges. We also came to realize that independent, one-off—also known as mom-and-pop—schools faced almost insurmountable hurdles in delivering high-quality academic instruction while running small businesses on tight margins. Consider the Omega School of Excellence, which in 2005 was operating in Dayton with 184 students. It received about $1.4 million a year from state and federal sources, which worked out to about $7,610 per pupil. In contrast, the Dayton public schools were operating at about $13,000 a child. That difference was the result of some $5,500 in local tax dollars going to district schools that charters such as Omega did not receive—and this on top of money for facilities and other outlays that were also denied to Ohio charters.[10]

From its meager per-pupil allocation, Omega had to pay for all staffing, food service, special education, facility, instructional materials (books, computers, etc.), and other expenses associated with running a school. Omega spent about $120,000 annually on facilities and utilities, and another $75,000 on food services. This meant it had about $1.2 million to spend on operations and instruction. It was required to contribute to the state retirement system—some 14 percent of salaries for every employee. Omega also offered basic health insurance and met the cost of federal Medicare payments. That meant the school paid about $645,000 in salaries and $175,000 in benefits. The result was that the average Omega administrator earned about $36,500 in 2005 while the average teacher made about $38,350. By contrast, Dayton public school (DPS) administrators earned about $68,500 and teachers about $50,550.[11]

Starting in July 2005, charter schools also had to pay fees to their sponsors, which cut further into their operating margins and was seen by many in the charter community as a harsh tax. It certainly created animosity between new sponsors and schools. More than once we heard complaints that "under ODE we received free sponsorship, and now we're paying you for sponsorship and you actually scrutinize our efforts far more than the state ever did." This was another reason for us to keep our sponsorship fees as low as possible, but it made for an unsustainable situation over the long run.

Quality sponsorship costs money that somebody has to pay. Other states have realized this and fund their authorizers in more rational (and less tightfisted) ways. For example, Florida provides sponsoring agencies 5 percent of revenue as do Colorado and Oklahoma. These dollars come directly from state to sponsors, not out of the schools' operating funds. In fact, the average payment structure for U.S. sponsors falls in the range of 3 percent to 5 percent of a school's per-pupil allotment.[12]

School districts also enjoyed economies of scale unavailable to most charters. With sixteen thousand students (in 2005), the DPS could order books, paper, technology, food, and so on at bulk discounts not accessible to a school with fewer than two hundred pupils. Scale also mattered when it came to administrative and back-office costs. Consider the school treasurer. A competent treasurer in Ohio could easily make $100,000 to $120,000 in 2005. (DPS paid $114,000.)

Yet state law obligated every charter school to employ a "certified" treasurer. Because the market for such individuals was, and remains, very tight, many charters complied by engaging a district treasurer to moonlight part-time. (In fact, this has become a very lucrative business for school treasurers in Ohio. One of them was reported to make $347,000 as treasurer for nine separate charters in 2009.[13]) A number of retired treasurers also worked with charters, but even on a part-time basis their per-pupil cost for treasurer services far exceeded that of districts.

Fiscal reporting burdens were also more onerous for charters. For example, they had to report their student counts to the state every month while districts did so twice a year. A charter school's monthly revenue could suddenly drop by several thousand dollars if, for example, a mother lost her job and moved her five children to another school. Districts also feel the pain of losing students but they adjust their spending once a year, not monthly. This matters hugely as teachers and other staff sign yearlong employment contracts, meaning that the charter school is on the hook for these costs whether pupils stay or leave.

Districts, of course, can also seek operating levies from local taxpayers to boost revenues beyond what the state affords them, while charters depend entirely on state and federal per-pupil allocations and whatever they can raise from philanthropy. (Some states—but not Ohio—give charter schools extra dollars in an effort to partially compensate for the absence of local dollars. Many now assist their charters with facility costs, too.)

A Strong Support Network

The economic challenges facing charter schools, especially the mom-and-pop variety, were not just problems for Fordham-sponsored schools. In 2009, Ohio had 309 charter schools, of which just under one hundred were independent operators. All but a handful served fewer than three hundred students and many enrolled fewer than two hundred. In fact, fully 75 percent of the charter schools operating in Ohio in 2009 served fewer than three hundred children apiece. Many ran on razor-thin margins.

In hindsight, many were financially doomed from the outset. In examining the causes of charter school closures in the United States, Brian Carpenter reported in 2008 that low enrollment was pivotal in the demise of almost three fourths of the 100 cases he studied. He advised school boards and authorizers to "strive for 300 students as the minimum desired enrollment for each school."[14] Yet most Ohio charters were—and are—below that threshold.

In studying charter schools nationally, Paul Hill of the University of Washington observed in 2010 that charter schools "often receive as little as 65 percent of the amount available to run regular public schools." While money doesn't assure educational success, it's needed to innovate successfully. Yet limits on the flow of money tilt the playing field and therefore dampen the formation of new schools of choice, Hill wrote, and "the only entities that can hope to compete are those that believe they can run effective schools with less money than district-run schools, or that are able to gain some form of subsidy, such as philanthropic contributions or donated labor."[15] The exception seemed to be schools associated with large, deep-pocketed national school-management organizations such as Edison and National Heritage Academies.

As noted earlier, Fordham had worked for years in Dayton to provide help to needy charter schools. Worried about the appearance, the legitimacy, and the politics of a charter sector dominated by big, out-of-state firms, many of them the for-profit kind, we felt it was especially important to develop and sustain a healthy crop of mom-and-pop schools with bona fide community roots. That's why we launched the Education Resource Center (ERC), originally at the Dayton Area Chamber of Commerce and later housed within Parents Advancing Choice in Education (PACE).

The concept was straightforward. We would help independent charter schools acquire benefits of scale by concentrating some of their needs and corresponding services in a single place, particularly their business management and other "back-office functions." This should, we thought, lead to lower-cost services for individual schools while improving the quality of those services for all of them. This, we expected, would reinforce their capacity to compete, stay viable economically, and, ultimately, deliver stronger academic achievement.

In 2003, as a result of political crosscurrents and message muddle within the PACE board, the ERC left PACE and became a stand-alone nonprofit organization named Keys to Improving Dayton Schools, Inc. (k.i.d.s.). At the outset, Fordham's Terry Ryan (as volunteer executive director) and Dayton businessman Doug Mangen ran the day-to-day operations of k.i.d.s. Fordham, with help from Dayton-area philanthropists and business leaders, including the former CEO of Copeland Industries, Matt Diggs, worked to raise money for the new venture.

About twenty charters were then operating in Dayton. Mangen surveyed their needs and learned that their most pressing challenges were improving financial management while boosting academic performance. It wasn't just record keeping and poor test scores. Several schools admitted that they were on the verge of financial collapse. The situation was captured in a memo from Ryan to the k.i.d.s. board in late 2003. "Early hopes for their transformative potential," he wrote, "are yielding to the realities of meager academic results, financial woes, leadership and governance difficulties, and political challenges. Local charter schools are largely consumed by issues of survival. As a result, they're not pointing the way toward educational excellence."[16]

The Omega School of Excellence was first to sign on with k.i.d.s. The copastors of the giant (2,500-parishioner) Omega Baptist Church, Vanessa and Daryl Ward, had founded the school in 2000 because they realized how awful the Dayton Public Schools had become. As Vanessa Ward recounted in an interview for this book, "We had many [parishioners] with school-age children, and there was no choice for them. They had to send their children to inferior schools and that was something affecting the families in our church."

She continued, "Routinely we would hear that, say 400 students had started as first-year students in high school, but only 180 were ultimately graduating. Hearing that, I couldn't sleep at night," she shared. The school's mission was straightforward. "Our focus is to prepare leaders for the twenty-first century," Reverend Ward explained in an interview during the Omega school's best days. "And that's a big task. The whole sense of getting students academically prepared plus emotionally and with a sense of commitment and responsibility to their community is of the essence for me. That's what I do all day in my ministry: empower people to make a difference. And I don't think you start when they graduate from high school, but you really start with them when they're young."[17]

Organized to serve fifth through eighth graders, Omega was modeled after the acclaimed Knowledge Is Power Program (KIPP) schools. At the outset, it had a KIPP-like intensive fifty-seven-hour instructional week with an emphasis on leadership, self-discipline, and academic achievement. Its graduates won scholarships to top local private high schools and several of the country's elite prep schools. But, like other one-off charters, Omega faced severe challenges on the business side. Vanessa Ward admitted that she lacked those skills. "This is a business. It's a start-up business. I think most persons who are in education don't necessarily come with those gifts—managing budgets and forecasting, insuring that you're making the best decisions fiscally to allow a start-up business to survive."[18] The Wards and their colleagues on the Omega board craved quality financial-management support, and k.i.d.s. was set up to help provide it to worthy but needy schools like this one.

For the 2003 to 2004 school year, k.i.d.s. agreed to provide Omega with treasurer and financial management support, and hired an accomplished former Dayton public schools treasurer to work as the school's treasurer. She left after six months, but by then k.i.d.s. was recruiting new talent to its financial management work as more schools queued up for such services. A partnership with the Wright State University accounting program was particularly fruitful. This was a good match since Wright State wanted to develop a "School Treasurer Track" for its finance students, and k.i.d.s. could help provide them with real-world experience. Gradually, k.i.d.s. put together a first-rate team of young school-finance talent led by Mangen. By mid-2005, it employed six staffers and three consultants who not only had the school-finance knowledge and appropriate state certifications but also possessed real expertise in navigating Ohio's Byzantine data-reporting systems.

At the start of the 2005 to 2006 school year, k.i.d.s. was serving eleven schools in four cities with a combined enrollment of about 1,860 students. The services generated about $400,000 in fees for "back-office" services. Fordham also subsidized k.i.d.s. to the tune of about $150,000 a year. According to the team of charter school experts that we engaged to evaluate the program: "Every school leader that participated in this process was both effusive and unanimous in their praise of the major and significant help and support provided by k.i.d.s. in the area of financial management. They lauded the work done by k.i.d.s. for their schools as 'outstanding,' 'invaluable,' 'excellent,' as well as indicating that in many ways k.i.d.s. provided the help necessary to keep them from closing."[19] Based on this success, the board of k.i.d.s., which included Fordham's Finn as well as Ryan, widened its mandate, adding academic and operating activities (e.g., food service support) and new schools in other cities. Too many Ohio charter schools were struggling academically as well as financially. K.i.d.s. wanted to see if it could build a full-fledged, high-quality, local charter management effort, something conspicuously lacking at scale in Ohio at that time. This service might even include running whole-school operations.

By now, Omega was facing serious academic challenges. Its initial success had been largely driven by Vanessa Ward's vision, energy, and commitment. But in 2005 she had to shoulder more church responsibilities when her husband became seriously ill. While she tended to him and their church, the academic leadership of Omega suffered. School heads came and went. Enrollment dropped and the school faltered. According to Vanessa Ward, "We never found a school leader that understood the (school's) vision."

Omega, at this point, needed not just outside fiscal expertise but a whole range of academic support. Such challenges, we were coming to discover, plagued many one-off charter schools, ones that depended overmuch on the vision and leadership of a single dynamic individual. When something happened to that person, the school too often spiraled downward. But k.i.d.s. did not have the resources to grow itself into a full-fledged charter management organization or purveyor of quality academic and management services. Neither did Fordham.

So in May 2005, k.i.d.s. submitted its own grant request to the Gates Foundation, seeking $970,000 over three years to support its expansion and to roll out a Dayton-based charter management organization. That plan also called for expanding k.i.d.s. financial, operational, and academic support services to develop evidence as to what does and does not work in charter school management while increasing the pool of human talent working on education and charter schools in Ohio.

By now, Ohio had several decent for-profit education management organizations (EMOs), including the New York–based Edison Learning (we sponsored their two schools in Dayton), the Michigan-based National Heritage Academies, and at least two strong e-school operators (the Ohio Virtual Academy and the Connections Academy). But the state had few quality nonprofit charter management organizations (CMOs) akin to California's High Tech High and Aspire; New York's Uncommon Schools and Achievement First, Washington, DC's Friendship Public Schools, and Houston's YES Prep. These models deliver results and offer the hope of "long-term sustainability—without indefinite philanthropic support."[20]

Ohio needed something similar and, when Gates agreed to assist k.i.d.s., its board immediately set out to identify a leader who could run such an endeavor and expand its mandate. Mangen declined the offer, saying he wanted to remain in a consulting role and work as an independent school treasurer. We knew what needed to be done and now we had the money to get started. But the project needed a full-time leader. K.i.d.s. conducted a national search for such a person and in early 2006 hired Dr. Robert Pohl as executive director. Pohl was a Notre Dame and Boston University graduate with a varied career in education. He had been a teacher in rural Mississippi and East Los Angeles, a Catholic school principal, a charter school developer, and president of the Santa Barbara, California, school board. In Dayton, he inherited a small yet complex school resource organization, which had contracts with thirteen schools for diverse services. More than half of the schools working with k.i.d.s. were also sponsored by Fordham.

These entwined relationships created both opportunities and problems. On the plus side, as sponsor we benefited from having competent people working in "our" schools as accountants and treasurers. They provided financial acumen and made sure the schools complied with state laws and audit requirements. This was especially important because, by then, Ohio prohibited a sponsor from authorizing any new schools if even one of its current schools was deemed "unauditable" by the state. Having financial experts in these schools also allowed us to speak authoritatively to state officials and possible external funders on behalf of the schools.

And it meant that the financial information we were receiving arrived in a standard format that utilized the same accounting categories. This made determining what was going on in the schools much easier and meant we could compare schools on such variables as per-pupil revenues and staffing costs. This was important in offering technical assistance that could benefit multiple schools because we knew what their common challenges actually were. It also meant we could share accurate financial numbers from real schools with other operators—like KIPP—we might want to recruit to Ohio. We could also provide modest grants to these schools with a high level of confidence that the money would actually be used as intended.

The most significant downside was the appearance, and sometimes the reality, of a conflict of interest. Fordham had helped to launch k.i.d.s. in 2003, long before we considered sponsoring charters in Ohio. We had given it hundreds of thousands of dollars in support, and two of its five volunteer board members were Fordham employees. Until Pohl came aboard in early 2006, k.i.d.s.' unpaid, part-time executive director was Terry Ryan, also Fordham's chief agent in Ohio. Despite the fact that all money flowed one way between Fordham and k.i.d.s., some could allege that Fordham was profiting from k.i.d.s. And Fordham-sponsored schools that purchased services from k.i.d.s.—oftentimes using grant dollars provided by Fordham—could claim (if the services were shoddy or there arose a conflict between school and k.i.d.s.) that they had been coerced into buying these services by their sponsor. It wasn't true, of course, but the sorry Harte Crossroads mess in Columbus illustrated the hazards.

The Fordham board was mindful of such risks. In 2004, before we even became a sponsor, Bruno Manno urged us to stop issuing grants to schools we would sponsor and to refrain from doing anything that could be seen as entangling us in their operations. It was only because of the profound needs facing mom-and-pop charters, the loyalty of these people to their community (the Wards were a vivid example), and the shortage of talented people available to help, that we sometimes skirted that sage advice.

The apparent conflict of interest between Fordham as sponsor and as grant maker generated a 2006 story in *Education Week* entitled "Fordham Connections to School That It Sponsors Spark Concerns." "There are a lot of interlocking relationship[s] here, and entanglements," remarked Henry Levin of Teachers College, Columbia University. "Without impugning motives, just institutionally, it doesn't sound proper to me. . . . You simply don't commingle public stewardship [sponsorship] with private commitments [grant making and support of k.i.d.s.]."[21]

In response, Finn noted that we had erected the necessary firewalls. We had established and widely disseminated a policy that made clear to schools we sponsored that "we will never tell you whom to hire and will not let you hire us, Fordham, to provide services. . . . We are precisely an independent accountability agent because we spun off the service-providing function to an independent organization [k.i.d.s.]."[22] Greg Richmond, the president of the National Association of Charter School Authorizers, explained that "if anything, it makes them more invested and more attentive." But he also cautioned that "if it were an ongoing activity, it would really start to complicate the lines of authority."[23]

The pressing needs facing our sponsored schools, as well as many other charter schools around Ohio, had inexorably drawn us closer to their day-to-day operations. As Finn remarked to the *Education Week* reporter, "If an important community organization sets out to run a charter school, and the school runs into trouble, my instinct is first to see if we can help them make it succeed."[24]

But the tension between our roles as judge and school doctor would never end. Surprisingly, the one school we thought, going into sponsorship, would need the least support, and could serve as a model for others, would turn out to be our greatest challenge. Cincinnati's W. E. B. DuBois Academy would test many of our assumptions about sponsorship and teach us some things we probably would have preferred not learning about the fragile complexity of the charter school enterprise.

Notes

1. "Community School Funding Report F2005," Ohio Department of Education, http://www.ode.state.oh.us/GD/Templates/Pages/ODE/ODEDetail.aspx?page =3&TopicRelationID=662&ContentID=42095&Content=79301
2. *State ex rel. Marc Dann, Attorney General v. Moraine Community School,* 07-CV-7921 (2008).
3. We criticized the attorney general's legal strategy in suing these four schools. In an article entitled "Dann: Right Struggle, Wrong Tactics" we observed that "there is a right way and many wrong ways to crack down on poorly performing charter schools. This week, Ohio's attorney general decided, unfortunately, that it's better to hold a few hundred children hostage in court than to let established law operate to cure what ails two Dayton-area charter schools. . . . This approach appears to be more of an attack on charter schools than a concerted effort to improve student achievement for Ohio's neediest children. Dann is in the right struggle but using the wrong tactics on the wrong battlefield." Thomas B. Fordham Foundation, "Dann: Right Struggle, Wrong Tactics," *Ohio Gadfly*, September 14, 2007, http://www.edexcellence.net/gadfly/ index.cfm?issue=393#a4322.
4. Thomas B. Fordham Foundation, "Sponsorship Accountability Report 2005–2006," October, 2005, 22.
5. Ibid., 19.
6. As part of the funding proposal to the Bill and Melinda Gates Foundation we committed to offering new schools free sponsorship for the first two years of their operation. Furthermore, as existing schools struggled to make their financial ends meet and deliver quality instruction we offered free or greatly reduced sponsorship to these schools.
7. Lou Whitmire, "Troubled Charter School Blames Gordon Firm," *Mansfield News Journal*, February 27, 2007, 1.
8. Ibid.
9. Jennifer Smith Richards, "Dead Schools Debt Mounts: Tally Stands at $1.6 Million; Students' Fates Uncertain," *Columbus Dispatch*, April 1, 2007, 1C.
10. Sheree Speakman and others, *Charter School Funding: Inequity's Next Frontier*, (Dayton, OH: Thomas B. Fordham Institute, 2005), 106.
11. Teacher salaries come from the ODE interactive Local Report Card, http://ilrc .ode.state.oh.us/Schools/default.asp.
12. National Association of Charter School Authorizers, "The State of Charter School Authorizing: 2008," Chicago, IL, July, 2009, 15, http://www .qualitycharters.org/files/public/Authorizing_Report_2008_FINrev_web.pdf.
13. Anthony Gottschlich, "Charter Schools Served by Treasurer Dogged by Fiscal Problems," *Dayton Daily News*, May 23, 2009.

14. Brian Carpenter, "Good to Gone: Five Lessons from Research about Charter Schools That Make the Leap . . . into Extinction," National Charter Schools Institute, 2008, www.nationalcharterschools.org/uploads/pdf/resource_20081104082833_Good%20to%20Gone.pdf.
15. Paul T. Hill, *Learning As We Go: Why School Choice Is Worth the Wait* (Stanford, CA, Hoover Institution Press, 2010), 37.
16. Terry Ryan, Memorandum to k.i.d.s. Board, November 2003.
17. Ibid.
18. Ibid.
19. Harold Kurtz and Donald Paolo, *Evaluation and Performance Report*, prepared for the k.i.d.s. School Resource Center at the request of the Thomas B. Fordham Foundation, December 2004, 5.
20. "Charter Management Organizations," New Schools Venture Fund, 2007, http://newschools.org/work/investment-strategy/charter-management-organizations.
21. Erik Robelen, "Fordham's Connections to School That It Sponsors Spark Concerns," *Education Week*, December 20, 2006.
22. Ibid.
23. Ibid.
24. Ibid.

8

An Education Tragedy

In his 2008 book on high-performing schools, *Sweating the Small Stuff: Inner-City Schools and the New Paternalism*, journalist David Whitman distilled the key practices used by America's most effective urban schools: telling students exactly what is expected of them; implementing a rigorous, college-prep curriculum aligned with state standards; regularly assessing pupil progress; building a culture of success; enforcing attendance; and shedding the constraints that hobble conventional schools.

In 2004, observers would have spotted nearly all of those elements in operation at Cincinnati's W. E. B. DuBois Academy. Its hard-charging leader, Wilson Willard, had created a culture that delivered academic results for needy children from some of the toughest neighborhoods in the city. DuBois was regularly among the top-scoring schools on state achievement tests and was named a "State Superintendent's School of Promise," a distinction given to those that exceed state and federal standards in low-income communities. Its record of success brought a 2005 visit by Governor Bob Taft. The school was lauded in the United State Senate as a praiseworthy example of closing achievement gaps and cited in the *Seattle Post-Intelligencer* as an example of why Washington voters should approve a charter school measure then on the ballot.

DuBois seemed to have it all, at least all that Whitman judged crucial: a longer school year and day, a "no excuses" culture for teachers and students, and a relentless focus on academic achievement. It also epitomized Whitman's definition of a "paternalistic" school: one that aims to change the lifestyles, values, goals, and expectations of its students. "We're the dominant social force in their lives," Willard explained to the *Cleveland Plain Dealer* in 2005. "We change the mindset, toward education."

Fordham and Wilson Willard

In October 2004, not long after Fordham took the sponsorship plunge, we were introduced to Wilson Willard by his godfather, Bishop Herbert Thompson, Jr., who led the Episcopal Diocese of Southern Ohio and had helped to launch the DuBois Academy five years earlier. Many in Thompson's diocese provided fiscal and professional support to the school. We already knew of its impressive academic record and were excited about the possibility of not only sponsoring this commendable educational institution—a sort of trophy school for a new authorizer—but also helping Willard to open additional schools.

In March 2005, as part of our due diligence efforts, Fordham trustees and staff met with him and several of his board members in Cincinnati to discuss sponsorship. Since its opening, the academy, like most of the state's charter schools, had been sponsored by the Ohio Department of Education (ODE). Because the legislature had ended ODE's role, it was looking for a new sponsor. Willard indicated that he wanted Fordham to take over sponsorship of DuBois and to authorize up to four additional schools that he planned to spin out from the DuBois experience. As DuBois then had a waiting list of over two hundred children, it made sense to help it branch out. Willard also noted that he had developed leadership talent ready to run schools of their own, and if he didn't open additional schools they would likely leave DuBois for other opportunities. And, of course, $450,000 apiece in federal start-up grants would help the new schools to launch. It all seemed to make sense.

Still, we sought an independent financial assessment of the W. E. B. DuBois Academy from Dayton-based school finance expert Doug Mangen and the Keys to Improving Dayton Schools, or k.i.d.s., organization. Mangen concluded that the school was viable but faced economic challenges. "The current fiscal health of the W. E. B. DuBois Academy is relatively stable," he reported. "The current equity position is weak, but plans are in place for improvement in [the next year]. The recurring and non-recurring cash flow is tight, but adequate to sustain the core educational programs. The financial history is grounded in an honest accounting of daily transactions; yet lacks in fiscal discipline and long-range financial planning."

"In summary," Mangen observed, "the [DuBois] Academy has met the immediate financial challenges of supporting the establishment of a high-quality education environment for its students. There are several immediate financial challenges and more are anticipated as the Academy begins to expand the number of schools. None of the current financial challenges appears to be fatal, but the financial risks will grow as the Academy continues to expand."

Plainly, DuBois and its planned offspring would face challenges, but these looked like nothing out of the ordinary. And the school's leaders seemed open to working with k.i.d.s. to improve their back-office operations. Moreover, DuBois had some loyal local philanthropic supporters and we believed that national funders like Gates, Walton, and the Charter School Growth Fund would be interested in supporting Willard's efforts to replicate success.

In consequence, Fordham and the W. E. B. DuBois Academy's governing board signed five-year contracts for sponsorship of DuBois and four additional schools, to take effect on July 1, 2005. We were truly excited about this partnership, particularly considering how many of the other "orphaned" schools we were adopting had developmental disabilities of various sorts. Less than a month later, though, Governor Taft signed into law House Bill 66, which (among many provisions) limited new charter start-ups to thirty more than then existed, thus voiding dozens of sponsorship contracts already executed across the state, including our agreements with DuBois's four new siblings.

When ODE held its lottery in July to determine winners and losers, the DuBois board received two of these coveted slots, thus gaining permission to launch the Veritas/Cesar Chavez Academy and the Cincinnati Speech and Reading Center. In August, after a crazy month of changing charter laws and rules, we became the official sponsor of the existing DuBois Academy and its two infant sister schools.

Unexpected Baggage

The ink on these contracts had no sooner dried than we started receiving complaints about Wilson Willard. Some of the allegations were made by anonymous callers to our office, and many seemed like little more than petty efforts to get even with him for dismissing teachers, reprimanding students, or making decisions that some people simply didn't like. But other complaints, shared in writing by people willing to sign their own names, were quite detailed.

Allegations ranged from not paying teachers for work they did, inappropriate language and conduct in front of children, sexual harassment of female teachers, and unfairly dismissing teachers, to complaints about Willard's basic approach to education and his speeding in a car with students aboard. One complainant, for example, said he rebuked pupils for cheering on another school's "step dance" team during a school competition. Willard was said to have told his students not to cheer for other teams. When asked, "What about good sportsmanship?" Willard reportedly replied, "That's for losers."

When appropriate, we followed up on all complaints and passed them along to the schools' governing board and, in a couple of instances, to Hamilton County Children's Services to investigate. We also regularly shared information with the ODE, whose staff reciprocated by passing information along to us that they had received about DuBois. We quickly started to accumulate serious legal bills as we sought counsel's guidance on how to proceed with some of the graver objections. We spoke with Willard directly about a number of them. His basic response was that these gripes and allegations were sour grapes from disgruntled employees or parents who didn't like his "my way or the highway" approach.

Willard's board steadfastly backed him. He delivered the academic goods and was committed to the schools. When visiting the DuBois Academy in the evenings or on weekends, one nearly always found him there with children. His schools seemed to be his life. Willard told the *Cincinnati Enquirer* in July 2005, "I will do whatever it takes to make these kids successful." We were disposed to believe him; so, apparently, were hundreds of families that sought entry for their daughters and sons into his schools. For every complaint we heard, many others sang Willard's praises.

Nevertheless, by November, the state auditor had yet to issue DuBois's financial audits from the previous two years, and we and the schools' board members had started to ask why. It was not unusual for such audits to take a year or more to complete, but two was beyond the norm. In early December, we contacted the auditor's office and asked about the delay. The initial school's files were not in good shape." A few weeks later, the auditor's office told us that DuBois was "unauditable" and "had become the subject of a special state financial investigation." This was the beginning of a lengthy drama that eventually resembled a Greek tragedy.

Over the next six months, myriad rumors, innuendos, and stories flew around Wilson Willard and his schools. A team of state auditors worked in the DuBois office every day. With each passing week, they increased the pressure on Willard, his administrative team, and the schools' governing board. On March 9, 2006, Willard told us that "the auditors came today wanting copies of all student enrollment records from the past three years." He noted that the auditors had been joined by officers from the Cincinnati Police Department with a warrant to examine student files. This was the start of a formal criminal investigation of Wilson Willard and possibly others at the school.

During this time, we were in regular communication with the schools' governing board and the lead investigator for the state auditor. In fact, the auditor sought information from us relating to our dealings with Willard.

Why did we take over sponsorship of DuBois from the state? Why did we agree to sponsor two more schools connected to DuBois? What sort of background checking did we do on the schools before deciding to sponsor them? How well did we know Willard? It was clear that the investigators were looking into something serious that antedated Fordham sponsorship. It was equally clear that they were trying to understand charter schools, the role of sponsors, and how the school-sponsor relationship is supposed to work under Ohio law.

We explained that, as sponsor, our legal relationship was with the governing board of the school and not with Wilson Willard personally. He was the governing board's employee. We also shared with the investigators copies of our sponsorship contracts with the DuBois governing board, and met with them on several occasions to answer questions and provide additional information, including a timeline of our relationship with Willard and his schools. We spelled out the financial incentives for Willard and his board wanting to open additional schools, notably the potential of federal start-up dollars amounting to as much as $450,000 for each new school—serious money in a state that kept its charters on such lean rations.

While cooperating with investigators, we also worked to help the DuBois governing board navigate the challenges swirling around Willard and the schools. Our primary point of contact was Edward Burdell, a successful and well-regarded Cincinnati businessman, a leader at the Episcopal Christ Church Cathedral, and a strong supporter of Willard. He and his fellow board members were volunteers who served the DuBois school and its offspring because they believed in its mission of providing needy "students with a superior education." They were, under state law, the ultimate body responsible for the schools—and for employing Willard.

During the early months of the investigation, we offered Burdell and his colleagues free technical assistance, including financial management support from k.i.d.s. where Doug Mangen was leading a team to clean up the school's financial records. K.i.d.s. was also working to put in place the fiscal procedures that the schools had sorely lacked. And the k.i.d.s. team was helping state auditors reconstruct DuBois's financial history from 2003 to 2005. Despite Mangen's original assurances to Fordham, the school's bookkeeping and record keeping were a shambles. The goal was to help it and the two new schools successfully navigate its fiscal challenges and to work with the state to resolve their fiscal problems. We kept reminding ourselves that 450-plus children and their families depended on these schools for their education—and that the academic results to date had been splendid.

Burdell was exasperated with the ongoing state audit. In an e-mail to us on March 16, 2006, he wrote: "We have spoken for some time about our frustration with the state audit process . . . the State process seems interminable—and as a board member—the equivalent of a snarled never ending string, with no end in sight. We recognize the responsibility they have to safeguard Ohio and its resources. Nonetheless, it seems that this audit has gone from conventional and cooperative to secretive and antagonistic. I cannot understand why simple, direct contact with the Governing Authority has been not possible. Thanks for your continuing support and assistance." Our effort to work with Burdell and his colleagues to keep the schools functioning was made more difficult by the increasingly troubling and erratic behavior of Wilson Willard. On the same day that Burdell vented his frustration about the auditors, we received three anonymous phone calls from DuBois teachers stating that Willard was at home with three students for the purpose of cleaning out his basement. We notified both the state auditor's office and Ed Burdell. In our e-mail to Burdell, we wrote that "we are receiving complaints from both parents and teachers, literally daily, on Wil's behavior. . . . We are concerned about these complaints, because if true, Wil is putting children at risk. This in turn puts you and your fellow board members at risk."

A few days later, we followed up with a note to Burdell encouraging him and his fellow board members to develop "if/then scenarios that can help you think through options before being forced to do so by events." We also noted that we "were seeking resumes from principal candidates and if you want access to these resumes as they come in, I'm certain they could be shared with you." In our minds, Willard needed to go or at least be placed on some form of administrative leave. Burdell and his colleagues didn't yet see it this way but they did take spending authority away from Willard and place it in the hands of the school treasurer and the board chair. Still, their loyalty to Willard ran deep. They saw him as the heart and soul of the schools—and as more victim than problem.

By May 2006, we were spending inordinate amounts of time and money on problems related to Willard and DuBois. Complaints rolled in daily about his behavior and we had been drawn into a new funding controversy between the schools and ODE. In the midst of the audit and investigation, the state was also trying to determine how much current funding should be going to these schools. Poor record keeping by DuBois made it hard for ODE to determine how many children actually attended the schools—and DuBois's extended year, although educationally desirable, didn't mesh well with Ohio's system for apportioning funds to charter schools.

In Ohio, charters are paid monthly for the students they educate and, as children come and go during a school year, they are funded in a prorated fashion—and never for more than 920 total hours of instruction no matter how many hours pupils are actually in class. DuBois kept children in school from 7:00 a.m. to 5:00 p.m., meaning they attended for more than

1,700 hours a year. In billing the state by the instructional hour, DuBois could use up the 920 hours in half a year. If a child transferred out part way through the year, the receiving school (if any) would have to educate him or her for the rest of the year without any additional state reimbursement. Perversely, DuBois benefited financially by having students leave mid-year. If students stayed the full year it cost the school, since, in effect, the school would be subsidizing the students' education beyond 920 hours. Predictably, all of this entails complicated formulae and data reporting. In this instance, ODE claimed that it had overpaid DuBois for students early in 2005 and now wanted school records and calendars to help determine what the correct amounts should be. The efforts of k.i.d.s. (paid for by Fordham) to provide answers was the only thing preventing the state from shutting off all funding to the DuBois schools.

A Serious Difference of Opinion

We were now in daily contact with Ed Burdell and school staff, as well as the k.i.d.s. team. Still, the DuBois schools were functioning academically, and it was clear that a number of exceptional young educators worked in them. These talented instructors were committed to educating children and delivering academic results. But they were wearying of the drama and many were on the verge of leaving. Hoping to hold onto the schools' teaching talent, we contacted staff at the Gates Foundation for help. Gates suggested a dynamic school leader who, they felt, would be interested in running the schools—provided that Willard was entirely out of the picture.

We shared this information—about possible Gates support and the opportunity to recruit a first-rate school leader—with Burdell in early May 2006, urging him and the board to place Willard on "voluntary administrative leave" and select a replacement sooner rather than later. But the DuBois board still refused to cut Willard loose. As we explained to our own board members, "They're sticking by Wil until/unless another shoe drops. Creating a prolonged, ambiguous, worrisome situation in which the school is quite unstable and people are exiting."

Our frustration was mounting. It seemed that the DuBois governing board would let Willard take the schools down before they'd replace him. One Fordham board member asked of the staff, "Are they blindly loyal to Wil or do they actually think the [likely] charges are false? Do they realize that standing by him, for either reason, may be the end of the school(s)?" Finn summed up our view in a May 9 e-mail: "Innocent until proven guilty . . . is an honorable old American value, but it's creating a limbo in this instance that I gather is very damaging to the school."

Despite the tensions and crosscurrents, we strove to resolve the new financial contretemps with ODE. The state claimed that the school had received overpayments of several hundred thousand dollars. We worked with state officials, Burdell, and Willard to devise an agreement for DuBois to repay these funds, or a fair portion of them, over time. It seemed that ODE was working in good faith, seeking a solution that would not kill the school. It and Fordham were working to save the top-performing charter school in Ohio, and we thought the DuBois board was on the same page.

Therefore, we were mightily surprised to receive a phone call on the morning of May 26, 2006, from Ed Burdell telling us that the governing authority had just passed a resolution closing the W. E. B. DuBois Academy effective that day unless the state gave it financial relief. This abrupt action was ill timed at best. To us, it seemed desperate, unwise, and unnecessary. In response, we issued a note, hand delivered to the office of the W. E. B. DuBois board chair: "As sponsor of the W. E. B. DuBois Academy, we find this course of action inappropriate and rash, and strongly urge the Governing Authority of the W. E. B. DuBois Academy swiftly to reconsider its decision. Abruptly closing the W. E. B. DuBois Academy more than a month before the end of the school year is plainly not in the best interest of the school's 450 students. We also believe that going forward with this decision will have serious legal, financial, and moral consequences that you may not have fully considered." This debate played out the next day on the front page of the *Cincinnati Enquirer*, which quoted Willard as saying that the state was seeking "as much as $3 million" in back payments. This was about five times anything ODE had suggested that the school actually owed, and Willard's comments—characteristically—made it appear as if DuBois were the victim. This, despite the fact that ODE had been working to help the school in a way that was both fair to DuBois and defensible to the state and its taxpayers.

This point was alluded to by Todd Hanes, then the senior department official in charge of charter schools, who told the *Enquirer* that "funding from the state for the year-round school was incorrectly calculated, and the school was overpaid." Hanes went on to note that no decision had been made as to how much money might have to be repaid. Our own comments were straightforward: "As sponsor, the Thomas B. Fordham Foundation's foremost concern is the welfare and education of the school pupils. Abruptly closing their school will obviously have grave, adverse effects on them."

The episode was now statewide news and discussion fodder for the national charter movement. The story being told most of the time was the one that Willard was spinning for his own benefit. The Center for Education Reform in Washington, DC, swallowed it verbatim and reported his tale that ODE "is clearly motivated for all the wrong reasons. We finally beat the local district [in achievement] and now there is a problem with our funding that has never been there before," Willard said. "We want to continue the excellence we've been able to achieve and the state is making it impossible. They changed the rules in the middle of the game and it's just not fair." The Center for Education Reform's news blurb recycled this line, even poking at Fordham by writing, "Sources say they [Fordham] are not backing the school in their fight with ODE. That would be a pity."

Although the DuBois board's rash decision was reversed and students missed no class time, this sequence destroyed the trust we had worked to build. Our relationship thereafter grew frostier and more legalistic with Burdell and his fellow board members. It was clear to us that Willard was still calling the shots and making key decisions for the schools. Considering the serious cloud he was under, this seemed downright irresponsible of the board. Willard was plainly the problem, yet he and the school's governing authority were pointing fingers at everybody but themselves. Disappointed and worried as we were, we nonetheless continued to work with Burdell and his colleagues to salvage the schools and continued to advocate for them in negotiating a settlement with the ODE. On July 31, 2006, we even issued an emergency grant of $50,000 to the W. E. B. DuBois Academy to pay for continued k.i.d.s. financial management services.

Time for Action

During the summer of 2006, we kept hearing rumors that Wilson Willard would be indicted. Many top teachers either were fired or quit as the schools' fiscal problems mounted. Few philanthropists were willing to aid a school under such a cloud. Leadership was in short supply, too. We spent a lot of time on-site and worried that DuBois and its sister schools were likely to be mere shells of their former selves when the new school year began.

Again, we urged the board to replace Willard with a new leader—and continued to offer leads on possible principals (including a solid internal candidate from the schools' teaching staff) who we thought would be interested in the job. We also suggested turning over school operations to an outside management organization. We even organized conversations for Burdell with Edison Schools and k.i.d.s. about the possibility of these organizations assuming responsibility for running the three schools. Finally, just before the start of the 2006 to 2007 school year, the DuBois board moved to replace Willard with a new school leader. Dianne Ebbs, who had herself chaired the board, now volunteered to serve as interim school director. She was a veteran Cincinnati educator and one-time mentor of Willard's who brought experience and credibility to the position. She agreed to work for a year without pay. Willard was made a paid advisor. This lasted until October 6 when he resigned. By then, we learned from the media, he had established himself in Connecticut as the principal of the New Beginnings Family Academy charter school in Bridgeport.

On October 25, 2006, Willard was indicted by a Hamilton County grand jury on six charges of theft, two charges of unauthorized use of property, two charges of tampering with records, and two charges of telecommunications fraud. Officials claimed, inter alia, that "Willard used $24,000 of state money to remodel bathrooms in his home." When word of his indictment came out, the parents of children at DuBois schools shared mixed views with reporters. Jashia Britten told the *Cincinnati Enquirer* that her ninth-grade daughter still hoped to graduate from the school.

"As long as the school is there and it's not threatening to close, my daughter will continue to come here," Britten said. "She's happy, and she's making A's and B's." Britten concluded that "the accusations facing Willard bring shame to an otherwise good school." Still, many parents remained loyal to him. "I think he was dedicated to the kids," said Sylvia Sally, a parent with three children in the school. "If there was a problem, a teacher wouldn't call you, he'd call you himself."

We were witnessing a genuine education tragedy. By the time of Willard's indictment, DuBois Academy and its sister schools were in free fall. Most of the top teachers had left. In October 2006, we sent school expert Joey Gustafson and her team into the DuBois Academy and its sister schools to evaluate their academic programs. She discovered that none of the three "has adhered to their original school models." Furthermore, she reported, the school curriculum "is nonspecific and there is not a common expectation regarding about specifically what is taught, when it is taught, and how it is taught. Due to the curriculum not being specific, it is unclear exactly how curriculum aligns to the Ohio State Standards."

The fact was that the curriculum had largely resided in Willard's head or, as one of his staff told us, "in his Palm Pilot." When Willard left, he took the schools' academic programs with him. In hindsight, we obviously should have been far more stringent in forcing the schools to put into written detail their academic programs before we signed them to sponsorship agreements in 2005. We simply took too much for granted.

On the first of November, we notified the chair of the governing boards that we were placing all three schools on probation for violating their charter contracts, specifically because they were not following the agreed-to education plan. Under Ohio law, the process of placing a charter school on "probation" is legalistic and procedural. We had to send a detailed letter spelling out the reasons for placing the schools on probation, the options available to them for getting off probation, and the steps we as sponsor would take should they not successfully meet the terms required to get out of probation.

Under state law, sponsors could place schools on probation for just one academic year, after which the sponsor must (1) suspend or close the school; (2) cancel the charter agreement, thus freeing the school to seek a new sponsor; or (3) end probation and move on. In response to our probation letter, the schools had ten business days to submit an action plan to resolve their problems or they would face immediate suspension and closure.

We were very clear about what the schools needed to produce to be exonerated:

- Academic audits by outside experts that showed, by March 15, 2007, the schools making "substantial progress" toward implementation of the curriculum as specified in their contract
- Outside monitoring of all state testing in spring 2007 (There had been allegations in the *Enquirer* and elsewhere that Willard may have cheated "on the statistics about student achievement.")
- Appropriate evidence of compliance with numerous state requirements, including criminal background checks on all staff and appropriate credentials for new teachers
- Necessary documents showing that the schools were making progress toward improved fiscal health and performance

Ed Burdell submitted the schools' action plans in mid-November. At the time, he told the *Enquirer* that he had shared a letter with Fordham stating, "We are confident that your representatives will see evidence of substantial progress as they review lesson plans, documentation of alignment of the curriculum to the Ohio standards, student work, professional development documentation and class schedules." We were giving the schools the opportunity to show that they could rebuild themselves after the chaos of the previous year, and Burdell, at least, seemed serious about seizing that opportunity, although privately we doubted they could pull it off.

During the rest of the 2006 to 2007 year, the DuBois schools made progress in complying with state law and cleaning up their finances (thanks largely to the efforts of k.i.d.s. and Doug Mangen). But as Fordham's director of sponsorship, Kathryn Mullen Upton, told the *Cincinnati Enquirer* in May 2007, despite hiring a treasurer, having their state tests monitored by independent observers, and making sundry other improvements, the DuBois schools were not making the academic progress that Fordham sought.

We thought seriously about closing the schools at the conclusion of the 2006 to 2007 year because they did not meet our educational expectations or their own contractual obligations with regard to curriculum, instruction, and student achievement. In fact, our review "found scant evidence of a coherent education program" at the schools. Charter school doctrine is clear that the sponsor's duty is to shutter schools that fail to deliver the necessary results. Yet we weren't certain that closing these schools was in the best interest of their pupils.

When we examined the alternative school options—both district and charter—that would be available to the five hundred or so children who would be stranded if the DuBois schools vanished, we found that their academic performance was woeful. They were worse, actually, than the DuBois schools, which had still received an "effective" rating when state report cards were issued in August 2006—and would be rated as "Continuous Improvement" after the 2006 to 2007 year. About 18,600 Cincinnati students attended schools with lower ratings. In other words, if we closed the DuBois schools, their pupils might very well wind up in schools that were even worse. Instead, we decided to negotiate an agreement with the DuBois leadership to keep two of the three schools open (DuBois and the Cincinnati Speech and Reading Center [CSRC]), while suspending operations at the third (Veritas/Cesar Chavez).

On May 4, 2007, we signed a Memorandum of Understanding with the chairs of the three schools' Governing Authorities that suspended Veritas and outlined a plan to remedy academic deficiencies at DuBois and CSRC. Key elements of that plan included the following:

1. Realigning the schools' grade levels to better target instruction
2. Acquiring strong new academic leadership, engaging an outside school management organization (like Edison or k.i.d.s.), or both to create and implement a revised academic program, with "said revision to be completed to the satisfaction of both parties by September 30, 2007"
3. Showing notable success in redesigning and implementing the new academic program (including curricular scope-and-sequence, formative assessments, etc.), as well as aligned assessments by December 31, 2007

From June through September, 2007, DuBois and CSRC made halting progress. They began the 2007 to 2008 year in better shape fiscally and organizationally. Yet when they presented their new education plan to us, it still didn't cut the mustard. After careful review, we concluded that it was not what their students deserved or needed, nor did it meet our standards of quality education. We also concluded, reluctantly and sadly, that after investing enormous amounts of time, energy, and money in this relationship and efforts to salvage and rebuild the schools, they were not likely to meet our standards anytime soon.

What to do? The schools didn't actually deserve to be closed down—and there was little chance that padlocking their doors would benefit their pupils. Yet they weren't good enough for us and we were profoundly weary of associating with them, offering advice that they ignored, and making demands and setting deadlines that they failed to meet. Nor could we afford—financially or in terms of staff time and board energy—to keep trying to help them fix themselves. Bottom line: after a rocky, star-crossed, two and a half years, the time had come to divorce them, to end a relationship that simply wasn't working and likely couldn't work.

In December 2007, we agreed with the schools' governing boards that they would close Veritas and seek a different sponsor for DuBois and CSRC. The two schools subsequently signed sponsorship agreements with a Cincinnati-based sponsor called Education Resource Consultants of Ohio (the same bottom-feeding authorizer that had taken on the Moraine Community School when it bolted Fordham sponsorship in 2006). Both schools, as we expected, then stumbled academically. At year's end (i.e., summer 2008), the W. E. B. DuBois Academy received a state rating of Academic Emergency while the CSRC was judged to be under Academic Watch.

Lessons Learned

On November 19, 2008, Wilson Willard pled guilty to five counts of theft and records tampering in connection with charges that he misused school funds and services to improve his home. He faced up to fourteen and a half years in prison. The *Enquirer* summed up the sad tale: "Willard, 39, founded the DuBois Academy in 2000 and, for several years, the school obtained Excellent ratings on Ohio school report cards. The school was year-round; children attended 10 hours a day, including after-school tutoring and activities. Willard frequently took the children out of town on trips. . . . DuBois has in recent years fallen in state ratings, now ranking in Academic Emergency, the lowest. The teachers Willard hired no longer work at the school; many parents have withdrawn their children. The school is run by different leaders and is structured differently." Despite the guilty plea, a seemingly unrepentant Willard told the newspaper "I don't feel like I'm guilty of anything. I understand [prosecutors'] interpretation of the law and the rules. But I also know what's in my heart." Nevertheless, in January 2009, regardless of whatever may have been in his heart, Willard was sentenced to four years in prison and ordered to pay more than $179,000 in restitution to the state of Ohio. Seven months later, the *Cincinnati Enquirer* reported that the W. E. B. DuBois Academy was "scheduled to become the first Cincinnati charter school to be shut down by the state for poor academics."

This saga was heartbreaking in so many ways, above all because so many children and families saw Willard and his schools as lifelines to good high schools and, ultimately, to college and a better life. Several superb educators left the DuBois family of schools and started schools of their own. (In 2008, we became sponsor of one of these, the Columbus Collegiate Academy.) Refugees from DuBois are now working in other charter, district, and private schools in Ohio and beyond. But what we had hoped could be an Ohio equivalent of KIPP or Amistad was gone. This hurt all the more because Cincinnati's and Ohio's other urban neighborhoods needed examples of successful schools that could make a difference for poor and underserved children.

Ohio's children craved schools like those profiled by David Whitman in *Sweating the Small Stuff*. Yet its highest-performing charter school imploded in a high-profile scandal that also wounded the Ohio charter movement as a whole. Instead of a success that charter supporters could point to for example and inspiration, it had become just another broken charter school that dashed expectations and killed hope.

For Fordham, this experience was humbling. *Education Week* captured our embarrassment in a piece in late 2006 headlined "School's Troubles Take Fordham by Surprise." It reminded readers of a front-page story from the *Cincinnati Enquirer* in July 2005 that had featured Willard in his prime. *Education Week* reported, "Mr. Willard was described as a 'role model for charter schools' by Terry Ryan, vice president for Ohio programs and policy at the Thomas B. Fordham Foundation."

Could we have done better at vetting Willard and the DuBois Academy in advance? Surely. But we might not have uncovered much more than we did when we first looked into the schools in 2004 and 2005. By all accounts, Wilson Willard and DuBois were golden. We now know that there was a dark side here that few saw or suspected—and some still don't see. Sometimes there are deep secrets that you don't get near in the course of visits and background checks. Willard resembled, in a small, southwestern Ohio way, Bernard Madoff and his $50 billion Ponzi scheme. As *The Wall Street Journal* observed of the latter scandal, "Financial scams are just one of the many forms of human gullibility—along with war (the Trojan Horse), politics (WMDs in Iraq), relationships (sexual seduction), pathological science (cold fusion), and medical fads." The paper might well have mentioned certain charter schools. We knew from the outset that sponsorship was risky and some schools might fail. We also knew that we might have to close some, which would surely be painful and costly. Did we envision a school blow-up as dramatic as DuBois? Of course not. Yet trying to reform public education and provide better options for needy children demands some willingness to take risks. This includes sometimes investing in individuals who show more promise than track record, and some of those investments will head south. With a bit of luck and a lot of judgment, more will pay off.

Notes

1. David Whitman, *Sweating the Small Stuff: Inner-City Schools and the New Paternalism*, (Dayton, OH: Thomas B. Fordham Institute, 2008), 259.
2. "Taft to Tour DuBois Academy," *Cincinnati Enquirer*, August 1, 2005, 3B.
3. Gregory Roberts, "Charter Schools: Battle Is Joined. Progress or a Step Backward? State's Voters Weigh Pros, Cons," *Seattle Post-Intelligencer*, October 27, 2004, A1.
4. Chris Sheridan, "Building the City's Entrepreneur Class; A Program to Teach Business Skills Grows into a Challenging Charter School," *Cleveland Plain Dealer*, June 14, 2005, B11.
5. Felix Hoover, "Bishop's Career Has Surmounted Adversity," *Columbus Dispatch*, June 3, 2005, 1G.
6. Doug Mangen, "Financial Assessment of the W. E. B. DuBois Academy," April 2005.
7. Ibid.
8. Complaint shared with the Thomas B. Fordham Foundation by Gaylen Blackwell of the Ohio Department of Education. The complaint was made by Terri S. Lewis and dated July 28, 2005.
9. Jennifer Mrozowski, "Building on Success," *Cincinnati Enquirer*, July 22, 2005, 1A.
10. Ed Burdell, e-mail to Terry Ryan and Kathryn Mullen Upton, March 16, 2006.
11. Terry Ryan, e-mail to Ed Burdell, March 16, 2006.
12. Ibid., March 20, 2006.
13. Chester E. Finn, Jr., e-mail to Fordham sponsorship committee members, May 9, 2006.
14. Ibid.
15. Terry Ryan, letter to Dianne Ebbs, Chairperson, Governing Authority, W. E. B. DuBois Academy, May 26, 2006.
16. Jennifer Mrozowski, "Top Charter School to Close," *Cincinnati Enquirer*, May 27, 2006, 1A.
17. Ibid.
18. Ibid.

19. "CER Newswire," Center for Education Reform, Washington, DC, May 31, 2006, http://www.edreform.com/index.cfm?fuseAction=document&documentID =2423&sectionID=58.
20. Linda Conner Lambeck, "New Beginnings Head Faces Indictment," *Connecticut Post Online*, October 25, 2006, http://nl.newsbank.com.
21. Sharon Coolidge, Jennifer Mrozowski, and Denise Smith Amos, "Charter School Founder Indicted," *Cincinnati Enquirer*, October 24, 2006, 1A.
22. Ibid.
23. JM Consulting, Inc., "W. E. B. DuBois Academy (WEBD), Cincinnati Speech & Reading Center (CSRIC), Veritas/Cesar Chavez Academy (Veritas)," March 7, 2007, 6.
24. Chester E. Finn, Jr., letter to Ed Burdell, Chairman, Governing Authority, W. E. B. DuBois Academy, November 1, 2006.
25. Rob Birk, "Charges Cast Doubt on Achievement Stats," *Cincinnati Enquirer*, October 26, 2006, 10C.
26. Jennifer Mrozowski, "DuBois School Board Plans to Leave Probation," *Cincinnati Enquirer*, November 17, 2006, 1C.
27. Denise Smith Amos, "DuBois Academy Taken Off Probation," *Cincinnati Enquirer*, May 19, 2007, 2B.
28. Jennifer Mrozowski, "Sponsor Slaps Probation on Three Charter Schools," *Cincinnati Enquirer*, November 2, 2006, 1C.
29. Under Ohio's accountability system, schools are given six academic ratings: "Excellent with Distinction" (in effect, A+), "Excellent" (A), "Effective" (B), "Continuous Improvement" (C), "Academic Watch" (D), and "Academic Emergency" (failing).
30. Denise Smith Amos, "Charter School Founder Pleads Guilty to 5 Charges," *Cincinnati Enquirer*, November 19, 2008, 1B.
31. Ibid.
32. Denise Smith Amos, "School Founder Gets 4 Years in Prison," *Cincinnati Enquirer*, January 8, 2009.
33. Denise Smith Amos, "Ordered to Close, W. E. B. DuBois Plans to Stay Open under Alias," *Cincinnati Enquirer*, August 31, 2009.
34. Erik W. Robelen, "School's Troubles Take Fordham by Surprise," *Education Week*, December 20, 2006.
35. Stephen Greenspan, "Why We Keep Falling for Financial Scams," *Wall Street Journal*, January 3–4, 2009, W1.

9

Polarization and Politics

I'm amazed at some of the really, really painful stories that six-year-olds and seven-year-olds are bringing to school, and the efforts of schools to deal with these things. I've gained more respect for traditional educators."[1] Thus Terry Ryan summed up for *Education Week's* Erik Robelen some of the many lessons learned by Fordham during its first two years of sponsorship. We were indeed humbled by the struggles—both our struggles and the schools' struggles—with the W. E. B. DuBois Academy and its sister schools; dismayed by the Moraine Community School dropping us for a less demanding sponsor; alarmed by the ongoing academic and fiscal failings of some of our other sponsored schools; and appalled by the periodic blow-ups of other charters across Ohio.

We also came to appreciate more fully the tremendous challenges associated with educating disadvantaged students in urban communities. And we realized—gradually—that charter schools, however well intentioned and earnest, aren't necessarily good at this. "Whereas charter boosters and advocates once supposed that charter schools would almost always turn out to be good schools," we wrote in *National Review Online* in late 2006, "reality showed that some are fantastic, some are abysmal, and many are hard to distinguish from the district schools to which they're meant to be alternatives. Merely hanging a 'charter' sign over a schoolhouse door frees it to be different but doesn't assure quality—or even differentness. Those running the school need to know what they are doing—and be good at doing it. Too many well-meaning (or, sometimes, greedy) folks set out to create charter schools that they aren't competent to run."[2] These lessons influenced not only our work as a charter sponsor but also our efforts to assist with the reforms of the Dayton public schools and other districts. And they affected what Fordham did and said as a national think tank. We found ourselves seeking a policy formula that still embraced choice but also held all schools to account for their academic results.

Charter Policy Repair

As we learned more about the tribulations of charter schools and the profound impact of public policy on their effectiveness, we strove harder than ever to repair Ohio's troubled charter program. Working within it clarified our understanding of the inconsistencies, gaps, and downright bad policies that continued to beset it. Initially, we and many others believed that the faster new schools could open, and the more youngsters they served, the better off everyone would be. As it became clear that too many schools were opening that didn't have a legitimate shot at success, and that too many of them then lingered in the decrepitude that the Ohio Department of Education, or ODE, termed "Academic Emergency," lawmakers responded by capping the charter program and dramatically slowing its growth.

This was a straightforward and politically justifiable reaction to the quality problems that beset the program. But to us it seemed shortsighted to halt the initiation of decent new school options when Ohio—especially urban Ohio—contained far too many failing schools, charter and district alike. In 2009, for example, about 97,000 children in Cincinnati, Cleveland, Columbus, and Dayton attended schools in "Academic Watch" or "Academic Emergency."

That compared with about 70,000 students in such low-performing schools across the rest of the state. The fact was that too many schools of both kinds were failing far too many of Ohio's neediest children. In Dayton in 2009, 63 percent of the 20,450 public school students (charter and district) attended schools rated D or F by the state. It was cold comfort that Dayton's charters were actually performing a bit better—that is, less badly—than district schools.

Ohio plainly needed more quality schools. Chartering remained a legitimate way to create and grow them. In pursuit of that objective, we reached out in late 2005 to people who counted most at the policy level: Governor Bob Taft, house speaker Jon Husted, senate president Bill Harris, and state superintendent Susan Tave Zelman. Teaming up with the Gates Foundation and the Walton Family Foundation, we suggested a high-profile conference on "Excellence in Ohio Charter Schools: What It Will Take and How to Get There."

The governor and both legislative leaders were Republicans who had played pivotal roles in building the state's charter school program, and they—along with Zelman—agreed to host such a "summit." Their invitation to it declared that "the overriding goal of charter schools in Ohio must be to dramatically increase student performance and narrow achievement gaps by providing high-quality education options for students and parents, particularly urban poor and minority families."[3] On November 17, 2005, more than two hundred education leaders attended the daylong event in Columbus. Its focus was squarely on school quality in general and improving the charter sector in particular. Speaker Husted noted in his opening remarks that "the top challenge for charter schools in Ohio will continue to be performance, making sure that children attending these schools are learning."[4] Governor Taft declared that "the best way to assure the charter school option remains strong and viable is a rigorous quality control program, timely intervention, and support."[5]

Tom Vander Ark, then Gates Foundation's lead education staffer, observed that although Gates had spent $141 million to help charter schools expand around the country, in Ohio "we have not identified high-quality operators serving low-income children that are in the process of or ready to replicate their success."[6] Former U.S. secretary of education (and Fordham board member) Rod Paige urged Ohio to implement a "retroactive fix" for quality standards, including dealing firmly with operators who never should have been involved in the system. He warned that "if we don't do this, we are creating a situation where we are working against ourselves."[7]

Other messages were also sounded, including admonitions that the charter sector and traditional school districts should stop fighting. "Rather than worrying about whether or not the children in our public or our charter schools are learning," Husted cautioned, "we're trying to vilify each other and win a political competition for market share rather than an educational competition for market share. That is not a helpful development in this state."[8] Fordham's Finn said that "the available options for families need to be good ones, whether they are district-operated or charter schools."[9]

The goal is to improve education for children, agreed Cathy Lund of the Walton Foundation. She predicted that "significant numbers of high quality charter schools combined with sound district reform will have a positive impact on improving the educational performance of all children."[10] Even some in the teacher unions expressed interest in trying to find common ground—or, at least, accepting the reality of competition. According to Pam Jackson, vice president of the Canton Professional Educators Association, "We don't want to fight with charters. We want to be competitive."[11]

The key challenges facing Ohio's charter school enterprise at this time were summarized by the *Cleveland Plain Dealer*: "Ohio's largest charter operator has been accused of violating state law by not testing students; a Cleveland charter was shut down because of fiscal mismanagement and traditional schools had better gains than charters on recent state academic reports."[12] Yet the answer was not to heap more regulations atop struggling schools. "In the name of accountability," Husted warned, "we're beginning to regulate, regulate, and regulate so that (charters) are losing their autonomy."[13]

The Corner Not Turned

One positive outcome of the summit was a serious move to start a new charter school organization in Ohio that would be dedicated to quality. Led by the National Alliance for Public Charter Schools and supported by Fordham, Gates, Walton, and the Pisces Foundation, this strenuous undertaking yielded the Ohio Alliance for Public Charter Schools. A second by-product of the summit was a critical analysis of Ohio's statutory framework for charter schools, requested by Taft, Harris, Husted, and Zelman and jointly undertaken by Fordham, the National Alliance for Public Charter Schools, and the National Association of Charter School Authorizers.

Issued in October 2006, that report offered seventeen recommendations to overhaul state policies in ways that would keep the "accountability/ autonomy" promise at the core of chartering, while strengthening Ohio's sponsorship system. It also sought fairer funding of charter schools and a lifting of caps that interfered with creation of more good ones.

At the time of the Columbus summit, Ohio had 299 charters overseen by 69 different sponsors, of which 8 were nonprofit organizations (responsible for 145 schools), 6 were county education service centers (85 schools, mostly associated with Lucas County), and 55 were local school districts (69 schools, many of them "cybercharters").

Under state law, just fifteen of these sponsors (Fordham among them) came under the authority of the Ohio Department of Education (ODE) while the remaining fifty-four were answerable to ODE only if they wanted to be. (Most, of course, did not.) To create a more coherent accountability system, the report's key recommendations included the following:

- A purge of low-performing schools
- Deterrents to "sponsor hopping" by operators of closed or on-probation schools
- Placement of all sponsors under contract with ODE and empowering that agency to discipline underperformers
- Assurance that charter funding be pushed closer to parity with district schools
- Payment for sponsorship with separate state dollars, rather than "taxing" schools
- Removal of caps on the number of charter schools[14]

Unreceptive Ears

The report was timed to influence the lame-duck legislative session in late 2006. Most observers expected Democratic Congressman Ted Strickland to be elected governor that November. His campaign statements showed that he was no fan of charter schools but a good friend of the teachers' unions and other establishment groups. It seemed smart to shape up the charter program and set some conditions for its future before he took office in January 2007. The report's authors briefed outgoing Governor Taft's education team, the house speaker, the senate president and Dr. Zelman. But we didn't gain a lot of traction.

Policymakers who had been eloquent at the summit a year earlier now indicated that it wasn't their job to solve the problems besetting the charter sector. Harris and Husted indicated that, in their view, the legislature had already made more progress in improving the charter program than our report acknowledged. (They cited the academic "death penalty" for failing schools, put in place in 2005, as well as other actions to tighten accountability on schools and sponsors.) They doubted that additional steps were really needed and worried that our report would embolden charter opponents—including the incoming governor—to seek more regulation rather than smarter accountability.

They also declared that charters could not expect to see more money anytime soon. The state simply didn't have it. Nor would they authorize a top-to-bottom review of all compliance and reporting requirements. The upshot was that Ohio's charters continued to operate with less money than district schools under a dysfunctional reporting system. And most of Ohio's sponsors remained free from oversight and accountability.

One reason legislative leaders didn't feel compelled to take firmer action to repair the program was that the state's charter community was, as usual, of at least two minds as to whether repairs were needed. Some viewed our report and its recommendations as positive, at least in public comments. "It constructively addresses the issue of charter school performance and accountability and it speaks clearly to the need for more adequate funding of charter education,"[15] said Ed Harrison, then chief executive of the Akron-based charter management organization White Hat.

Others saw it very differently. A charter principal in Cincinnati railed against what he saw as a double standard: "We have public schools and public school districts that have been in Academic Emergency for two years or more, and they have not closed public school districts. Why should a charter school be treated any differently?"[16]

The teacher unions and their allies also flayed the proposed new policies and spending: "Ohio's charter school program certainly needs to 'turn the corner to quality,'" said the Coalition for Public Education, "but these recommendations would very likely result in more tax dollars being wasted in underperforming charter schools."[17] Democratic state senator Teresa Fedor, a longtime charter critic, told the *Cleveland Plain Dealer* that the "study was misleading and lacked credibility because it was ordered by the state's pro-charter Republican leadership and compiled by unabashed charter school supporters."[18]

A few modest improvements were made during the lame duck session. Taft signed House Bill 276 into law in late December 2006, widening the exemption to Ohio's charter cap to enable the well-regarded Knowledge Is Power Program (KIPP) and other high-performing nonprofit charter networks to operate schools in the state. The bill also created an incentive for districts to make their facilities available to high-quality charter schools by allowing for inclusion of the charters' performance data in their academic report cards. That arrangement created a win-win situation whereby high-performing charters could obtain facilities, and districts could benefit academically (by counting charter student test scores within their own) and financially, by putting unused facilities to use. (This policy innovation impressed charter advocates in California, Colorado, and Texas, which sought to incorporate versions of it into their laws.)

House Bill 79, signed by Governor Taft in the waning days of his term, also added a few of the accountability measures recommended in *Turning the Corner to Quality*, including language that deterred sponsor hopping, and strengthened academic accountability for persistently failing schools. But most of our seventeen suggestions went nowhere.

Others also found their policy guidance ignored. In early 2007, the Ohio Board of Education received a remarkable 102-page report from Achieve, Inc., a national education reform group led by governors and CEOs. With funding from the Gates Foundation, Achieve had commissioned McKinsey & Company, one of the world's foremost consulting firms, to examine key aspects of Ohio's education system and report on how the Buckeye State could become a world leader in education by 2015.

McKinsey called for providing "all students with access to high-quality, publicly-funded school options."[19] It urged the state to shutter the worst schools, encourage high-performing networks and schools to open, strengthen the accountability of sponsors, and confer funding parity (including facilities funding) on solid performers. Similar pleas came from the Ohio Grantmakers Forum, representing many of the state's leading private foundations. Yet state leaders pretty much disregarded all this input— even though much of it had been solicited by them. They had other fish to fry and interests to protect.

Warring Interests

When it came to charter schools in Ohio, two competing interests typically turned what should have been the sensible center into a bloody battlefield. On one side was organized labor (the teacher unions and their allies, often including school boards, administrators, and colleges of education). On the other side was business, represented (at least in charter school debates) by profit-making management companies, above all David Brennan's Akron-based White Hat firm. Both sides regarded the politics of charter schools as a zero-sum game in which a gain by either must come at the expense of the other.

This led to prolabor Democrats supporting anticharter legislation while probusiness Republicans protected extant school operators and resisted accountability moves that they saw as anticharter. Neither side really understood, nor much cared about, the role of sponsors as quality controllers. Democrats viewed them as ineffectual middlemen at best; at worst, as agents of the big-school operators. Republicans may have better understood the sponsors' role but did nothing to strengthen their hand in imposing quality control on schools and operators.

Year in and year out the favorite target of charter critics was Brennan's White Hat firm, which in 2008 to 2009 operated thirty schools enrolling 11,483 students and received $79.2 million in state funds. The political and public relations pounding that White Hat absorbed, along with weak academic results in many of its schools, appeared to be exacting a toll. Just a year earlier, White Hat schools enrolled 15,673 pupils and took in $109 million in state funds. Almost overnight, the company had seen its enrollment and revenues shrink by more than a quarter.

The *Columbus Dispatch* once referred to White Hat's head as "the godfather of Ohio's charter" schools and acknowledged that "Brennan, the most influential non-elected Ohioan in the last two decades, almost single-handedly changed the face of education through political connections, campaign contributions, and the sheer force of his ideas and personality."[20]

It's true. Nobody mattered more to the birth of Ohio's charter school program than David Brennan. Critics of that program, like the unions and the George Soros-backed, Cleveland-based Policy Matters, contended that he was driven by greed and that his charter efforts were part of a larger agenda to privatize public education. They also claimed that his personal business interests came at the expense of school transparency and accountability—and that procharter politicians and complicit sponsors simply clicked their heels and did his bidding.

This line of attack was summarized by Policy Matters executive director Amy Hanauer in late 2008:

> Take, for instance, the career of Sally Perz, the Republican who sponsored Ohio's initial charter school legislation. Perz left political office to become a lobbyist for the University of Toledo, where she was a member of the university's Charter School Council. This council approved White Hat's proposal for a statewide virtual (online) charter school, for which the school received $32 million in taxpayer money. Perz's daughter, Allison, later formed a non-profit that became the Ohio Council of Community Schools. Sally Perz, who had moved on to become a private consultant, was paid $61,200 from her daughter's agency in the first year, and was also paid by White Hat Management as a lobbyist. Later, 19 White Hat schools hired the Ohio Council of Community Schools as their sponsor, paying it $405,000. Four other firms hired Sally Perz as a lobbyist and hired Allison's organization as their sponsor. These cozy relationships may help explain the weak oversight that for-profit charters have received in Ohio.[21]

Such political and financial entanglements between operators and sponsors were also decried by the *Toledo Blade* and *Cleveland Plain Dealer* in 2006. The former editorialized that "when charter schools emerged on the Ohio educational scene more than a decade ago, they were hailed by many, including this newspaper, as a potentially innovative and lower-cost alternative to the state's disturbingly mediocre public school system. What was not envisioned is that charter schools would become cash repositories to be siphoned of sponsorship and management fees, in some cases by politically connected individuals."[22]

The *Plain Dealer* added that "Ohio faces another potential obstacle— a seemingly built-in conflict of interest involving the state's first line of oversight. Charter school sponsors are often chosen and paid by the very schools they are supposed to be holding accountable." Of the thirty-one White Hat schools in 2008, "records show that 19 are now sponsored by the Ohio Council of Community Schools [OCCS], a Toledo group headed by the daughter of a pro-charter former state legislator who, for most of the last two years, was a registered lobbyist for both White Hat and OCCS."[23]

It was because of such dubious relationships—as well as far too many weak schools—that we pushed hard for changes to state law to strengthen school accountability. We enlisted all the allies we could. Mostly, though, we lost these battles. Self-interested opposition within the charter community was part of the reason, as was enmity toward charter schools in general. Partisanship played a role, too, as did the fractured leadership and mixed motives of Ohio's charter movement. But bad earlier policy decisions turned out to be a surprisingly large part of the problem. Like a big ship that is hard to turn in stormy seas if it has a faulty rudder and misfiring engines, Ohio's charter program proved difficult to redirect in no small part because of the policy mistakes already embedded in it.

Sponsors, for example, are responsible under state law for monitoring schools' performance and ultimately making life or death decisions about their futures. Yet in Ohio the money flows not from sponsor to school but from school to sponsor. In other words, the entity responsible for monitoring school quality is paid directly by the schools it oversees and ultimately judges. Thus, the checks and balances are systemically out of whack, as if the Securities and Exchange Commission operated on a percentage of each dollar earned by the Wall Street firms that it is supposed to oversee.

When Ohio constructed its charter system this way, it was trying to create accountability on the cheap. Charter schools were expected to deliver more for less; hence the idea of spending additional tax dollars to support their regulators had no traction with conservative lawmakers. Nor did school operators have any incentive to seek the creation of independent oversight agencies that were serious about quality and truly empowered to redirect or close troubled schools. This produced a weak, even perverse, accountability system that in turn furnished charter foes with additional ammunition.

Some Ohio charter supporters even pooh-poohed the very idea of external accountability. They asserted that the marketplace was the only real accountability mechanism anybody needed. Brennan colorfully summed up this view for the *Columbus Dispatch* in 2005: "I trust parents. I've learned to trust the unemployed, prostitute, minority mother more than any educrat I've ever met in my life."[24]

Larger-Than-Life Target

Brennan was and remains a true original, a brilliant political operator, bona fide education reformer, and self-interested profit seeker, all rolled into one. He believes fervently in the power of market forces and school choice to improve education. He believes that competition ultimately makes all schools better. And he believes that education is the pathway out of poverty.

In furtherance of those beliefs, he has donated millions to education causes, including Catholic education, and he almost single-handedly created the Cleveland voucher program. He was pivotal in defending it all the way to the U.S. Supreme Court. He also cares deeply about Akron. The *Columbus Dispatch* reported that he donated "$50 million from his own pocket"[25] to help rebuild that city's downtown.

Brennan made a fortune as a lawyer and industrialist long before he got into education reform, and there's no reason to think he ventured into the latter primarily in order to enrich himself further. But he also saw White Hat as a business that, like any business, should make money, not lose it. In his view, parents—with the help of a little marketing and advertising—would determine which schools to send their children to and, if they're content with the education that results, and the operator can also pocket a few bucks while delivering that education, everybody benefits, including incentives and financing for operators to expand the supply of schools that satisfy parents.

This attitude toward schooling combined with Brennan's rare clout in Columbus—at least on the GOP side of the aisle—to render him an obvious target for charter foes. (Brennan is a large and visible target, being tall and imposing—and sporting a striking white Stetson in most gatherings.) He was, and remains, the state's foremost charter school bogeyman, and critics have worked hard to give him, his company, and for-profit education management in general bad names. What's more, they've largely succeeded, and it's in no small part for that reason that legislation has repeatedly been filed to make it illegal for for-profit operators to run schools in the Buckeye State. (In his 2009 biennium budget, Governor Ted Strickland again sought to ban for-profit operators from having anything to do with Ohio charters; as in 2007, this initiative was rebuffed by Republicans lawmakers.)

Our own frustration with Brennan, and with many others in Ohio's charter school space, arose from our conviction that those schools must be accountable to the public's interest in quality education as well as to market demand. Parents, we knew from firsthand experience as a sponsor, are often unfussy consumers, at least with regard to academic quality. Many will keep their children in a school that doesn't deliver much learning so long as they feel it is safer than their other options, or that people in the school are friendly, or that it is conveniently located in relation to their home or workplace. Without demeaning such considerations—what parent doesn't put safety first when it comes to his or her daughters and sons?—we also recognize that charters are public schools, that the nation is academically at risk, and that taxpayers deserve to invest their hard-earned dollars in schools where children actually learn.

In the No Child Left Behind era, *every* public school, charter and district alike, is held to account for its academic results—and corrective actions of various kinds are supposed to be taken when those results are unsatisfactory.[26] We are not alone in believing that academic results matter as much as parent choice, indeed that there's a healthy tension between those two considerations. Just as academic achievement in the absence of parent satisfaction doesn't get the job done—even a fine school must close if nobody wants to attend it—so contented parents without academic results are insufficient for society's needs.

The public has an interest in ensuring that all of its children are educated—and in the charter sphere it's the sponsor's duty to ensure that this happens. That core belief has powered Fordham's many collisions with other charter supporters. Too many of them—sadly, this is also true of the traditional district sector—don't believe that all children can learn much. Too many believe that schools are doing their job if they keep children off the streets and out of danger, and parents contented and at work. Many of these people also despise standardized tests and results-based accountability. What matters to them is customer satisfaction and teacher happiness. We beg to differ.

In Ohio, we kept finding ourselves stuck between two immovable forces. On one side were choice proponents like Brennan with whom we disagreed about matters of school accountability. On the other side were the teacher unions and their allies who simply wanted to abolish charters and other forms of school choice. The latter truly revolted us, because most of them were public employees in whom society has vested enormous trust to do right by its next generation. Yet most of the time—all the time, it seemed, when charters and choice were involved—they were self-interested, keen to obliterate all threats to their membership, their power, and their purse.

In 2006, the Ohio Education Association shared with its members a paper entitled "The Current State of Ohio's Charter School Program." It declared that "the charter school program in Ohio is nothing more than a thinly veiled attempt to 'dismantle' public education."[27] It noted that "charter schools have reduced union-represented bargaining unit positions. . . . The total number of traditional public school personnel, excluding administrators, lost to charter schools is calculated to be (in 2004) 4,782."[28] It then estimated that 9,374 union jobs would be lost by the end of 2006.

The animosity between the unions and Brennan was palpable. In discussing White Hat in 2005, the late Tom Mooney, then head of the Ohio Federation of Teachers, declared that "these schools are not independent, nonprofit entities. They are captive creatures; they are company stores." The head of the Ohio Education Association added that "there are legislators at the state and federal level who would like to see every school building privatized. There is big, big money involved. Just look at what David Brennan has received for the few schools he's got."[29]

These critics despised—and feared—him in particular, but their beef extended to all for-profit school operators. The venom hurled by the teachers union at Dayton superintendent James Williams in 1998 when he considered outsourcing the operations of five troubled schools to Edison was their customary modus operandi. David Brennan simply personified the threat.

The Changing Political Landscape

During their four debates in 2006, both Democratic gubernatorial candidate Ted Strickland and Republican Kenneth Blackwell talked charters. Their positions were polar opposites. Blackwell repeatedly voiced his commitment to such schools and argued for opening the gates to as many as the market could sustain. Strickland called charters "a rip-off." He argued that "there are people operating these schools getting rich and they're doing so on the backs of our children."[30] Each candidate accused the other of serving someone other than children, with Blackwell charging Strickland with being a puppet of teacher unions and Strickland painting Blackwell as a hired gun for Brennan and the profiteers.

In November 2006, Strickland was elected by a landslide, receiving 60 percent of the vote to Blackwell's 37 percent—the worst showing by an Ohio GOP gubernatorial candidate since 1912. True to his campaign rhetoric, Governor Strickland's first budget, released in March 2007, went after charter schools on several fronts. Indeed, it would have dismantled the state's charter program by creating a moratorium on all new schools and imposing a slew of regulatory provisions on those that already existed, good and bad alike.

He would even have barred high performers like KIPP from the state, prohibited for-profit operators of every sort (not just White Hat but also such generally solid outfits as National Heritage Academies, K12, Connections Academy, and Edison), reduced charter funding in several ways, and required charters to follow all laws and regulations that applied to district schools, thus ending their already limited freedom to be different.

House speaker Jon Husted rallied the legislature, still controlled by Republicans in both chambers, to defend the charter program. Procharter rallies were held across the state, including one in Dayton that attracted six hundred people. According to the *Dayton Daily News*, "Many who attended wore T-shirts with messages such as 'I love my charter school,' and held handmade signs that read 'save our schools.'"[31]

The house budget approved by a unanimous and bipartisan vote in June 2007—the first time this had happened since 1955—deleted most of the governor's charter provisions but did little to improve the charter program. In effect, it maintained the messy and mediocre status quo.

Notes

1. Erik W. Robelen, "A Think Tank Takes the Plunge," *Education Week*, December 20, 2006.
2. Chester E. Finn, Jr., "All Aboard the Charters?" *NR/Digital*, October 9, 2006.
3. Governor Taft, President Harris, Speaker Husted, and Superintendent Zelman, "Invitation to All Excellence in Ohio Charter Schools Summit Attendees," October 2006.
4. Andrew Welsh-Huggins, "Conference Highlights. Efforts to Improve Charter Schools," Associated Press, November 17, 2005.
5. Scott Elliott, "Tougher Rules for Charter Schools? Conference Aims to Improve Their Academic Performance," *Dayton Daily News*, November 18, 2005.
6. Associated Press, "Conference Highlights."
7. Gongwer Ohio News Service, "Speakers at Charter School Conference Underscore Need for Quality, Accountability Standards," November 17, 2005.
8. Ibid.
9. Ibid.
10. Ibid.
11. Paul E. Kostyu, "Charter Schools Good, Have Problems, Say Advocates," Copley News Service, November 18, 2005.
12. Reginald Fields, "Support Qualified at Charter School Conference," *Cleveland Plain Dealer*, November 18, 2005.
13. Jennifer Smith Richards, "Charter Schools' Freedoms May Slip Away—State Might Tighten Rules in the Interest of Improved Scores," *Columbus Dispatch*, November 18, 2005, 6E.
14. Thomas B. Fordham Institute, National Alliance for Public Charter Schools, National Association of Charter School Authorizers; with Louann Bierlein Palmer, Michelle Godard Terrell, Bryan C. Hassel, and C. Peter Svahn, *Turning the Corner to Quality: Policy Guidelines for Strengthening Ohio's Charter Schools*, October 2006.
15. Scott Stephens, "Backers Scrutinize Charter Schools," *Cleveland Plain Dealer*, October 12, 2006, http://www.cleveland.com/charter/plaindealer/index.ssf?/charter/more/1160642046211680.html.
16. Jennifer Mrozowski, "Too Many Charter Schools Failing," *Cincinnati Enquirer*, October 12, 2006.
17. Ibid.
18. Stephens, "Backers Scrutinize Charter Schools."
19. Achieve, "Creating a World-Class Education System in Ohio," December 2006, http://www.achieve.org/files/World_Class_Edu_Ohio_FINAL.pdf.
20. Joe Hallett, "Man Behind Charter Schools Movement Is a Force to Be Reckoned With," *Columbus Dispatch*, October 20, 2005, 7B.
21. Amy Hanauer, "Profits and Privatization: The Ohio Experience," in *Keeping the Promise? The Debate over Charter Schools*, ed. Leigh Dingerson, Barbara Miner, Bob Peterson, and Stephanie Walters, 45–46 (Milwaukee, WI: Rethinking Schools, 2008).

22. Editorial, "A Political Education," *Toledo Blade*, July 10, 2006, A8.

23. Bob Paynter, Sandra Livingston, and Scott Stephens, "Who's Profiting from Ohio's Charter Schools?" *Cleveland Plain Dealer*, March 19, 2006, A1.

24. Quoted in Joe Hallett, "Self-Appointed Superintendent Industrialist Builds Ninth-Largest School District Using Political Clout," *Columbus Dispatch*, October 23, 2005.

25. Hallett, "Man Behind Charter Schools."

26. In Ohio, NCLB had few teeth when it came to forcing troubled charter schools to improve. This was due to the fact that few sponsors took this federal law very seriously, and the state's department of education was more concerned with paper compliance than with forcing real changes—for example, replacing principals and teachers—in failed schools.

27. Andy Jewell, "The Current State of Ohio's Charter School Program," Ohio Education Association, Columbus, OH, 2006,1.

28. Ibid., 12.

29. Catherine Candisky and Randy Ludlow, "Taxpayer-Funded Charter Schools Profitable," *Columbus Dispatch*, October 23, 2005, 9A.

30. Quoted in Scott Stephens, "Gubernatorial Debate—Round Two," *Cleveland Plain Dealer*, September 21, 2006, A1.

31. Scott Elliott, "Parents, Students Rallying for Charters," *Dayton Daily News*, April 19, 2007.

10

The Rest of the Story

In 2009, Governor Strickland and his allies relaunched the policy and budgetary attacks they had mounted two years earlier—but this time with a Democratic majority in the house. The 2008 elections had been good to their party in Ohio as well as nationally. Although the GOP retained a 21 to 12 majority in the senate, four of the five statewide offices were now in Democratic hands. The biennial budget proposed by the governor in early February 2009 would have nailed shut the coffin for Ohio's charter school program. We summarized that threat for the *Akron Beacon Journal* in these words:

> Ohio's charter schools certainly need attention and the governor has a good idea or two here—making all charter "sponsors" accountable, for example. But while purporting to cure this patient, Strickland would actually deprive it of vital limbs and organs. His budget would severely worsen the funding inequities between charter and district schools. And he would heavily increase the regulatory burden on all charters, good, bad, and indifferent. In barring "for profit" school operators, he again fails to distinguish between shady managers of squalid schools and outstanding providers of quality education. That both may be profit-seeking is beside the point. Put it all together, and it's hard to picture any high-octane charter operator wanting to work in Ohio. These operations will instead go to states that welcome and support them. This would be a blow to needy children and families.[1]

The hostility toward charter schools on the part of Strickland and his fellow Ohio Democrats was not their party's national position. In Washington and in many other states and cities, some of America's foremost charter advocates were Democrats, beginning with President Barack Obama and education secretary Arne Duncan. Democratic mayors have been especially strong for quality charter schools, notably Richard Daley in Chicago, Adrian Fenty in Washington, DC, Corey Booker in Newark, and Bart

Peterson, the former mayor of Indianapolis. During the 2008 campaign, then-senator Obama picked—of all places—Dayton to highlight his own support for charters. But it wasn't just election talk. In the midst of Strickland's attempts to chip away at charters, Obama told a *Cleveland Plain Dealer* reporter in March 2009 that "we've got to experiment with ways to provide a better education experience for our kids, and some charters are doing outstanding jobs."[2]

The Charter Effect

Whether the topic is choice, teacher preparation, school funding, or just about anything else, education politics in the Buckeye State in 2009 still revolved around money and adult interests. The charter school debate is still seen by partisans on both sides as a zero-sum game: the size of the money pie is fixed, they believe, and if charters get a larger slice the district sector is sure to get less—and vice versa. There's no doubt that the economic downturn and stressed budgets of 2008 to 2009 and 2009 to 2010 have made everyone nervous and possessive when it comes to state funding. Over the past decade, however, Ohio's public education pie has grown by hundreds of millions of dollars. From 1997 to 2008, Buckeye State expenditures per pupil rose from $7,500 to more than $10,000 in constant dollars.[3] Nor do those numbers reflect the additional billions spent by the state and local school districts on new facilities during this period.

Yet many in the traditional public education sector insisted that charters had harmed them, their districts, and their 1.7 million students.[4] By providing alternative education options to 4 percent of Ohio pupils, most of them refugees from troubled district schools, it was alleged, charters had hurt the other 96 percent by draining away resources that were rightfully theirs. Such critics chose not to notice how much the total pie had grown—far more and far faster than its charter slice. Governor Strickland was the most prominent Ohioan to buy into this argument but he was not alone.

If charter schools haven't hurt public education in Ohio, they haven't repaired it, either. The RAND Corporation issued a major study on charter performance in eight states in early 2009 that found "no evidence in any of the locations [including Ohio] that charter schools are negatively affecting the achievement of nearby traditional public schools."[5] On the other hand, RAND continued, "There is also little evidence of a positive competitive impact on nearby [district students]."[6] In short, charters in Ohio could be called a wash in terms of pupil achievement.

Then why bother with them? For one thing, charter schools have led to some positive developments that are not easily measured by standardized tests. They have, for example, drawn organizations and individuals, who otherwise might not be involved, into urban education issues. They have certainly drawn fresh talent into schools serving needy children. And they have engaged parents and children who felt alienated in district schools. Recalling John H. Patterson and his efforts to improve Dayton in the early twentieth century, really good charter schools have also immersed community leaders and philanthropists in urban education, often in leadership roles. We've seen this in every Ohio city where Fordham has been involved. Among the handful of schools that we sponsor, for example, board members include business and civic leaders, prominent clergy, a former legislator, a sitting federal judge, academics, philanthropists, and former public school officials.

These men and women have committed themselves to the betterment of their communities and those communities' children by sitting on nonprofit charter boards and they expect nothing in return. Their experience of working directly with schools serving needy youngsters has led to deeper understanding of the challenges facing urban educators. Many charter school board members also have strong relationships with traditional districts and their leaders. They reject the zero-sum view of charter-district competition and they do not allow adult interests and institutional jealousies to determine how they approach education in their communities. They really do "put children first."

Charters have also drawn individuals into teaching and school leadership who otherwise wouldn't or couldn't be involved. Several of the schools we sponsored in 2009 had teachers who emerged from the acclaimed Teach for America Program. They are graduates of top universities who, under Ohio's regular licensure rules, could not work in district schools without jumping through costly and time-consuming—and, say most, pointless—certification hoops. So they work in charter schools.

Charters have also attracted school leaders from unconventional places, people like Reverend Vanessa Ward—a Johns Hopkins graduate in international studies—who founded the Omega School of Excellence in Dayton with her husband, Georgetown Law School graduate Daryl Ward. Top young school leaders like Andrew Boy—who founded the Columbus Collegiate Academy after completing the Boston-based Building Excellent Schools program—and Hannah Powell, who now runs the state's first KIPP school, were attracted into public education because they wanted to lead high-performing urban schools. Judy Hennessey, a retired district superintendent from a wealthy Dayton suburb, took the reins of the Dayton Early College Academy as its principal and helped to turn that charter school into one of Dayton's best high schools. These school leaders see closing the achievement gap as a social justice issue and charter leadership as a way to help bring about a better society.

Charter schools have also engaged parents and children alienated by traditional district schools. This helps to explain why thousands of charter parents and students gathered on Ohio's statehouse lawn in 2007 and again in 2009 to protest proposed funding cuts to their schools. By giving families an education choice, they also gain a voice, and this is a powerful thing for those who have long felt ignored and ill served.

The Situation in Dayton

In Dayton, where we and many others had invested so much time, energy, hope, and money in building and trying to strengthen charter schools, academic results remained mixed. It was scant consolation to see the district producing scores that were even worse. Of the fifty-five Dayton schools to receive academic ratings from the Ohio Department of Education in 2009, thirty-one got the equivalent of D or F marks (56 percent). Only two—both charter schools—earned an A. More remarkable, 61 percent of the students in Dayton charters in 2008 to 2009 were in schools rated A, B, or C by the state, while 74 percent of Dayton's public school students attended schools rated D or F.

Ohio's charters could hardly be held up as models of educational excellence, but in Dayton they were inching education in a better direction. Yet K through 12 education in our hometown remained generally mediocre to dismal. Despite the emergence of a lively school marketplace via charters, private scholarships such as PACE, and, since 2006, a state-financed voucher program, the traditional system remained sorely troubled. For a few years, led by the reform-minded Kids First board majority, DPS had shown gains, with achievement ticking upward from 2002 through 2006.[7] Then the wheels again fell off the bus.

In late 2005, the Kids First team forfeited its majority when one member lost to a union-backed candidate. Months later, a second one left the board and the Kids First team was down to two—board president Gail Littlejohn and vice president Yvonne Isaacs. In May 2007, the district failed to pass a significant levy. This triggered painful cost cutting and finger pointing, as well as tensions among board members and the larger community. By year's end, Littlejohn, the dynamo who had led the district for the previous six years, resigned and moved to Texas.

Charter schools again became scapegoats for the district's woes. It didn't help that the state and Dayton Public Schools (DPS) were embroiled in a dispute over discrepancies in charter enrollment figures, which, the district claimed, had wrongly deprived it of $7.1 million.[8] Board president Yvonne Isaacs told a meeting of national education journalists that "over the nine years of charter schools in Dayton the district has lost $283 million that was transferred to charter schools," which, she alleged, had scored lower than traditional public schools. "It would not have cost us nearly that much to educate 6,000 students, we believe."[9]

Though district officials never acknowledge this and perhaps never will, in one sense Dayton public schools (DPS) benefited financially every time a child left for a charter school. Imagine that each DPS pupil arrives with a backpack of cash, worth about $13,619 (in 2008 figures), representing the total taxpayer contribution to that youngster's education. That backpack actually contains three wallets. One represents federal dollars (about $2,315); the second consists of state dollars ($6,128); and the third contains local tax dollars generated by Daytonians via levies ($5,176).

If that child then leaves DPS for a charter school, the backpack that accompanies her move is considerably lighter, because the third wallet stays with the district. The child takes only the state and federal dollars into the charter school, totaling about $8,500.[10] The local portion remains behind. So while total district revenues decline as charters grow, district resources per remaining pupil continue to rise. Indeed, if charters drew off every student but one, that last, lonely DPS pupil would be the beneficiary of tens of millions of dollars in public spending.

Yet even Littlejohn retroactively fingered charter schools for the travails of DPS. In a 2008 interview for this book, she said the challenges of reforming the system and balancing its budget had grown more difficult "with charter schools seemingly popping up in every neighborhood. The competition got pretty brutal sometimes. . . . Unfortunately," she continued, "they've been a bad thing for the city."[11]

Such criticism may be in part an effort to deflect attention from the DPS academic achievement decline that resumed in 2006 and accelerated in 2007 and 2008, a time when district funding averaged more than $13,600 per pupil. As for enrollment competition, charter school growth in Dayton peaked at around 6,400 in 2006, although the city's larger demographic decline continued apace. As a result, total public school enrollments (charter and district combined) shrank by some 3,380 pupils from 2005 to 2009 (see Table 10.1).[12]

Fewer charter schools were operating in Dayton in 2006 than in 2005 and fewer still in 2008 and 2009 (see Figure 10.1). This decline was predictable in light of the statewide cap on new charters, the enactment of tougher accountability standards including automatic closure for deeply troubled schools, a lean economy, and the simple fact that there were fewer Dayton children to go around.

Table 10.1   Student enrollment in Dayton public schools (DPS) and Dayton charters (2000–2009)

Year	DPS enrollment	No. of Dayton students enrolled in a charter	Total public school enrollment in Dayton	% of public school students in Dayton enrolled in charters
2000	24,916	1,230	26,146	5
2001	22,590	3,048	25,638	12
2002	20,147	3,573	23,720	15
2003	18,163	4,770	22,933	21
2004	17,593	5,135	22,728	23
2005	16,710	6,291	23,001	27
2006	16,348	6,403	22,751	28
2007	15,825	6,036	21,861	28
2008	15,023	6,252	21,275	29
2009	14,393	5,228	19,621	27

Source: Ohio Department of Education interactive Local Report Card (http://ilrc.ode.state.oh.us).

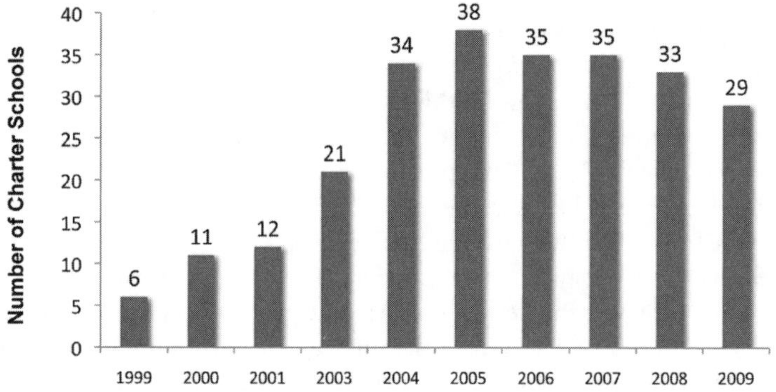

Figure 10.1   Charter schools operating in Dayton (1999–2009)
Source: Ohio Department of Education interactive Local Report Card (http://ilrc.state.oh.us).

In a fresh review of DPS in 2008, the Council of the Great City Schools did not blame charters for the district's travails. Instead, the council observed that "the school board began to change as critical members decided not to seek re-election. The administration may have taken its eye off the ball and lost its focus. The public, possibly sensing district uncertainty and the loss of energy, voted against the bond issue that might have prevented some of the recent programmatic upheavals. The result of these developments, in combination, was largely responsible, in our minds, for the slowdown in student achievement between 2006 and 2008."[13] The council, in fact, recommended that DPS "design a process by which high-achieving charter schools that are interested in reaffiliating with the school district can do so on terms that allow the charters flexibility that regular schools may not have."[14] But that recommendation was immediately followed by "accelerate efforts to improve relations between the school district's leadership and the teachers' union."[15] In practice, the latter admonition likely precluded taking the former admonition seriously.

Competition or Cooperation?

Most of the challenges facing DPS were shared by the charters. In visiting both kinds of schools across the city, one heard the same complaints: we don't have the resources we need; we lack great teachers in our classrooms; we need better leadership; we need to do something about children's home lives because they are bringing impossible problems to the schools; we need more discipline, and so on. Educators in both sectors were toiling to make a difference, and in both sectors could be found some—not enough—terrific people doing great work against daunting odds.

Dayton was still losing families to its suburbs and far beyond, and the demographic crash worsened as the brutal economy of 2008 to 2010 took its toll on jobs and families. The children who remained were largely poor, minority, and struggling mightily. Such challenges beset every sector of education, including private schools and charters as well as the traditional district. Nevertheless, DPS did, boast an awesome collection of gorgeous new buildings, courtesy of local and state taxpayers (and the tobacco companies). Charters had nothing of the sort, which explained our 2008 decision to help terminate the East End Community School as a charter and assist it in merging into the district—in return for use of one of those grand new schoolhouses.

East End had had facility problems since its inception in 2002. When the church in which it rented space terminated that arrangement, the school had nowhere satisfactory to conduct class. And so, in May 2008, with our blessing and technical assistance, its board reached an agreement with DPS leaders whereby East End would cease operating as an independent charter, and its pupils would be encouraged to enroll in the district's newly built Ruskin Elementary School. Many teachers and staff from East End subsequently took positions in the new school. This arrangement allowed the district to fill an otherwise underutilized new building with students while enabling East End's pupils to move into a suitable facility.

Merger into the district was not an option for the Omega School of Excellence, which we had supported and encouraged since its birth in 1999. Never really large enough to be viable as a stand-alone school, Omega was simply unable to make its economics work any longer, despite substantial subsidies over the years from Fordham and other Dayton-area philanthropists and supporters and much support from the church itself. After much discussion and soul-searching, it was agreed jointly by the school's leadership (Vanessa and Daryl Ward and the board) and Fordham that trying to continue operating just made no financial sense. Opening in fall 2008 would put children (and staff) at risk of losing their school midyear, thus creating real disruption in their lives. The Omega board authorized a formal resolution ceasing the school's operations at the end of 2007 to 2008, and we blessed it and helped to explain the decision to parents, students, teachers, and the larger community.

This was painful for all concerned. Vanessa Ward, the school's founder and mainspring, captured the feelings in an interview for this book: "I have grieved so greatly over this school. I still have a lot of pain when I talk about it."[16] Despite the pain, she still believes that "closing was the right decision. Trying to keep it going would have ended up in some negative ways. As it was, we helped children find new schools and teachers find new jobs. It was done with integrity."[17]

Reverend Ward notes, though, that while it lasted, Omega succeeded for many children. "We did good things for a number of kids. A number of them are in college or on their way. So many of these children are first-time college students in their families," she says. "That gives me some consolation. My heart is still heavy that there are so many more children in Dayton who deserve better and are not getting it."[18]

Omega's demise also dealt a mortal blow to our effort to create in k.i.d.s. a nonprofit school management organization that could run successful schools across Dayton and southwestern Ohio. We had raised money from the Gates Foundation in 2005—it was spent by 2008—to develop k.i.d.s., but, with the closure of Omega, the k.i.d.s. organization also folded. It could not overcome the double whammy of Omega's demise and the decision by Doug Mangen, the Dayton businessman who had built the k.i.d.s. financial management services, to spin these off into his own company.

That had been the only part of k.i.d.s. that generated serious revenues. Although Omega was a terrific beta site for k.i.d.s. to develop its own CMO skills, with the Gates subsidy spent and no more fee-paying schools under the k.i.d.s. umbrella, the venture had no means of balancing its budget.

Both organizations were also wounded by the national economic downturn that reduced Fordham's endowment—and those of many others—by more than one third. This fiscal misery made it far harder to raise money for a struggling school and a fledgling CMO that faced uncertain futures even in flush times. In seeking financial assistance for them, we were challenged by one funder: "Do we support a school or support the organizations that are feeding and clothing many of the children in the school?" Human capital proved problematic, too. Finding and keeping great talent to work in Dayton's charter sector was a nut that k.i.d.s. never cracked. And when it engaged the services of really capable individuals, they swiftly proved to be in great demand elsewhere. Mangen was one example; so was Hannah Powell, the able young educator—a Teach for America alumna—who served as Omega's principal during much of 2008. She was wooed away by the KIPP program to open a new school—which we also sponsored—in Columbus.

Under these circumstances, k.i.d.s. could not survive, despite Ohio's obvious ongoing need for more great urban schools. We had to shelve our hope for a Dayton-based CMO. There are, to be sure, several national charter outfits—for example, Edison Learning, National Heritage Academies, KIPP—operating in Ohio, and some of them do good work. But what this approach neglects, and what Ohio (and many other places) still needs, are mechanisms for strengthening mom-and-pop schools like Omega, which have deep roots in their communities yet lack the educational and management capacity necessary to sustain success.

Another Blown Opportunity

For a time in 2007 and 2008, Dayton saw halting attempts by district officials and charter supporters to find ways to collaborate. Seeking to encourage this, in April 2007 we shared a document with community leaders that sketched a "Portfolio Governance Approach to Meeting the Needs of All Dayton Children." This idea, long favored in concept by Gail Littlejohn, called for steps to improve "the quality of Dayton's educational marketplace."

We noted that the emergence of such a marketplace had, overall, been a positive development that gave poor families choices, catalyzed some innovative school models, and provided competition. But "for some families, the creation of this school marketplace has come with serious short-term losses for their children. Too many families have learned about the consequences of choosing bad schools only through the bitter experience of having their children languish in a failing school for months or even years."[19]

Building on the experience of cities like Chicago, New York, and Houston, we again urged Dayton to consider a "tight-loose" system of school management. We explained that this meant "tight" as to results but "loose" with regard to operations. We noted that other cities were diversifying their school portfolios so that districts were no longer just owner-operators of their own schools but also "quality control agents" for portfolios of different types of schools. We again explained the basic charter concept and how it could be embraced and turned to advantage by DPS. And we offered to help the district to understand and embark on sponsorship if it were so inclined, even to see our own Dayton charters—two of them the largest and sturdiest in town—become part of this effort if a deal could be worked out that vouchsafed their autonomy.[20]

Summarizing the case for such collaboration, we wrote that "Dayton's families want school choice, but they also want to support the community and the community's efforts to improve public education. They also want and deserve the best possible education for their children. It is for this reason that Dayton should take seriously the idea of bringing all of its quality public schools under one community-based oversight structure committed to a portfolio approach to school governance."[21] We sketched five possible benefits of such an approach, including a chance for Dayton to emerge as an education-reform leader rather than a basket case; a reduction in local hostilities; a shot at financial help from national foundations; a way of purging bad schools; and a terrific opportunity for engaging many sectors of the community in a joint revitalization effort.

In June 2007, a meeting was convened at the University of Dayton to discuss these ideas and other ways for DPS and the charter community to collaborate. Participants included house speaker Jon Husted, district superintendent Percy Mack, Gail Littlejohn, and some fifty-five education, political, and business leaders. They gathered just a month after the district failed to pass its operating levy and was cutting jobs.

Unfortunately, what could have been a rare occasion for rapprochement and constructive engagement wound up as mainly an airing of boasts and grievances. As captured by a local journalist, Mack "touted the district's recent gains in test scores and graduation rate and new school options such as single gender schools. He also said Dayton had been badly hurt by its impending budget cuts [precipitated by the recent levy failure]."[22] Senator Tom Roberts, a Democrat, blamed state funding for the problems that Dayton and other urban schools faced. "Policies at the state level continue to perpetuate a lack of resources for these schools,"[23] he told the gathering.

Dayton thus missed another opportunity to do something bold, an opportunity summed up by one of the city's top charter leaders, Ann Higdon, who observed, "We have all the issues of a major metro area, but we are small enough to have a chance to get our arms around that problem."[24] But there was too much accumulated mistrust between those who called themselves charter supporters and those who called themselves district supporters. There wasn't enough goodwill to bridge that divide. District and charter partisans both thought they could come out ahead in the legislature, and therefore neither thought they needed the other. Changes within the DPS leadership worsened the standoff, as it was widely known that Percy Mack was seeking a job elsewhere. (In June 2008—after six years at the DPS helm—he accepted a position in South Carolina.) Besides all that, both district and charters faced pressing fiscal and academic problems that consumed their time and attention. People rightfully worried about taking their eye off the bottom line—the success of their individual organizations.

Change Is Slow in Coming

Mack was replaced by Kurt Stanic, a veteran Ohio superintendent, who came into the job in August 2008 with the goal of passing a school levy three months later. He succeeded, too, even though this was a far smaller levy than voters had turned down in May 2007. Still, it gave the district a bit of breathing room. In an early 2009 interview for this book, Stanic declared that he did not intend to be the long-term leader of DPS, and in fact he would be replaced by a new superintendent at the conclusion of the 2009 to 2010 school year. At fifty-seven, and with a widely lauded career in public education already behind him, Stanic said he saw his job in Dayton as focusing the district squarely on student performance, putting a strong leadership team in place, and setting the conditions for the long-term health of the district's finances.

When it came to charter schools, Stanic said he didn't take them into account in his planning but was open to cooperating with decent ones. He predicted that in time the district would eventually sponsor a half-dozen or so successful charters. He also reached out to the business community and cultivated relationships with civic leaders. He asked for their help in passing the levy and regularly communicated with them to avoid "the district's past mistakes in dealing with business leaders."[25]

For Stanic, the district's greatest challenge wasn't charter schools but poverty. "Poverty is everything," he said, adding, "the economy has tanked since I've been here."[26] (Dayton had a poverty rate for five- to seventeen-year-olds of 32.8 percent in 2005 and the numbers surely worsened in 2008 and 2009 as businesses closed and unemployment and homelessness rose.)

Despite all those challenges, Stanic believed that good schools could help children learn, even those living in poverty. We shared this belief and continued to help the district when we could while also supporting the schools we sponsored and trying to woo proven operators to Ohio. We also strove to collaborate with partners in Dayton and beyond who were committed to creating better educational options for needy families and children. Considering how many in Ohio viewed Fordham as a conservative think tank with Republican proclivities, it was ironic—and a bit exhilarating—to discover after the 2008 election how much of our reform agenda now aligned with that of President Obama and Secretary Duncan.

Indeed, we felt as if we could have scripted Obama's July 24, 2009, speech on education, when he declared,

> We can't hold charter schools to lower standards than traditional public schools. If a charter school is falling short year after year, it should be shut down. But if we're holding charter schools accountable and if we are holding them to high standards of excellence, then I believe they can be a force for innovation in our public schools. And that's why I've encouraged states to lift caps on the number of charter schools allowed—something being done in Louisiana, Indiana, and across the country. And that's why we will reward states that pursue rigorous and accountable charter schools with Race to the Top Fund grants.[27]

In 2010 the president and the U.S. Secretary of Education Arne Duncan went on to press all states, including Ohio, to increase their support for charter schools as a condition for Race to the Top funds.

Notes

1. Terry Ryan, "Strickland Pushes Flabby Evidence," *Akron Beacon Journal*, February 10, 2009.
2. Stephen Koff, "Obama Backs Charter Schools for Cleveland," *Cleveland Plain Dealer*, March 11, 2009, http://blog.cleveland.com/openers/2009/03/obama_backs_charter_schools_fo.html.
3. Public Impact and the University of Dayton, "Fund the Child: Bringing Equity, Autonomy, and Portability to Ohio School Finance," Thomas B. Fordham Institute, Dayton, OH, March 2008, 6.
4. Leigh Dingerson, "Reclaiming the Education Charter: Ohio's Experiment with Charter Schooling," *Center for Community Change*, November 2008, 2.
5. Ron Zimmer and others, "Charter Schools in Eight States: Effects on Achievement, Attainment, Integration, and Completion," *Rand Education*, 2009, xv.
6. Ibid.

7. "Next Steps in the Improvement of the Dayton Public Schools," Report of the Strategic Support Team of the Council of the Great City Schools, Washington, DC, Fall 2008, 6.

8. Anthony Gottschlich, "Dayton Schools Will Get $7.1 Million to Settle Enrollment Dispute," *Dayton Daily News*, May 5, 2009, A3.

9. Scott Elliott, "Official: Bad Charters Hurt Schools; Dayton School Board President Tells Seminar Choice in Education Can Be Good, but Underperforming Charter Schools Rob Students," *Dayton Daily News*, October 7, 2007, A4.

10. Conflicting state laws make for some commingling of state and local money, resulting in some local dollars accompanying children into charter schools. In Dayton, though, such sums are minimal.

11. Gail Littlejohn, interview by Mike Lafferty, 2008.

12. Some of those children moved to private schools through the state's Ed Choice voucher program.

13. "Next Steps," 7.

14. Ibid., 8.

15. Ibid.

16. Vanessa Ward, interview by Mike Lafferty, May 2009.

17. Ibid.

18. Ibid.

19. "Put the Education of Children First: A Portfolio Governance Approach to Meeting the Needs of all Dayton Children," Thomas B. Fordham Institute, Dayton, OH, April 5, 2007.

20. In August 2009, the Center on Reinventing Public Education at the University of Washington published "Performance Management in Portfolio School Districts." This report identified the characteristics of portfolio districts: (1) concentration of dollars and decision making at the school level; (2) free movement of money, students, and educators from the less- to more-productive schools and instructional programs; (3) strategic use of educationally relevant community resources; (4) rewards to educators for high performance; (5) openness to promising ideas, people, and organizations, whether they belong to the school district or exist in independent organizations; and (6) an environment of support for both new and existing schools.

21. Ibid.

22. Scott Elliott, "Dayton Schools' Future Focus of Summit," *Dayton Daily News*, June 12, 2007, A4.

23. Ibid.

24. Ibid.

25. Ibid.

26. Ibid.

27. "Remarks by the President on Education," The White House, July 24, 2009.

11

Hard Lessons

Even with the support and encouragement of a president and an education secretary bent on fundamental change in this realm, education reform at ground level is no walk in the park. On the loftier plateau of research, policy, and philosophy, we at Fordham probably know as much about it as anyone. And we would not deny that it's encouraging and stimulating to work out, in the world of theory, just which reform elements need to be melded with which other elements in which ways, and to explain how, when all these are perfectly lined up, like chessmen on a grand master's board, one's victory over ignorance is all but assured.

And yet our work in Ohio has brought us into intimate contact with reality and shown us time and again how different that world is from the planet of theory. A waggish friend once defined a "think tank" as "a place where reality is studied to see if it accords with theory." Fordham's think-tank side occasionally matches that definition. Yet our efforts in the Buckeye State have vividly demonstrated—not just once, but time and again—how reality can be a crucible in which theory melts beyond easy recognition.

Viewed from ground level and through the lens of reality, we see that, despite all the theorizing and reforming, all the studies and analyses, all the lawmaking and new money, no American state or city has yet figured out how to educate all of its children to high levels, especially the poorest and neediest among them. What reformers are discovering across the nation— this is especially vivid in Ohio—is that, however inspired and comprehensive a policy formula may appear, the actual circumstances of kids' lives and community dynamics limit its effectiveness. And that's without even getting into the institutional rigidities and political obstacles that impede its thorough application.

As readers will have noted, a recurring theme in these pages has been the naïveté with which we entered into programs, activities, and relationships that, with the benefit of hindsight, we can see were far gnarlier than we realized at the time. Although we're worldly grownups, not easily misled, we admit to sometimes having donned spectacles that made things look more straightforward than they turned out to be. We wanted to believe that people would do what they said; that organizations possessed greater resilience and capacity than they did; that policymakers and practitioners could be counted upon to stay true to the interests of children; that institutional habits could be altered; that personal self-interest could be suppressed on behalf of the common weal; and that our own goodwill and hard work would be reciprocated by others.

OK, call us credulous, even gullible. We won't contest the charge. We're surely wiser now; not less principled but a tad less confident; no less determined but a bit less certain that the faithful application of our theories will yield the results we seek.

In this concluding chapter, we summarize eighteen of the most important lessons we've distilled from the reality of our work in Ohio these dozen years, lessons with relevance far beyond the borders of the Buckeye State. They're lessons that, one might say, theorists have derived from reality, which means that they're lessons that resonate in the domains of policy and practice alike. And while Ohio may present a distinctive package of challenges, particularly in the charter school realm, every one of those challenges has echoes and reflections in other states across this broad land. (Admittedly, the lesson in some instances is "For Pete's sake, don't do what Ohio did!")

The first five lessons illuminate the context of education reform today, particularly in regard to charters and schools of choice. The next seven describe elements that we've found to be essential to a successful system of high-performing schools of choice. The final six discuss problems worth trying to solve and obstacles that need to be surmounted.

The Context for Today's Education Reformers

1. Placing a "charter" sign over a schoolhouse door doesn't guarantee educational excellence—or much of anything, when you get right down to it, except a public educational institution with the *opportunity* to be different. That doesn't mean it will make good use of that opportunity or that the ways in which it's different will prove sound, efficacious, and durable. Far too many American charter schools produce results no better—and sometimes worse—than the failed district schools to which they're meant to be alternatives. Too many states—Ohio among them—allowed their zeal to launch charters to

trump their judgment as to which would-be school operators had decent odds of yielding solid achievement.

Yet the charter phenomenon is here to stay. During 2009 to 2010, more than 1.5 million youngsters attended over 4,900 public charter schools in 39 states and the District of Columbia, almost 4 percent of all children enrolled in public schools nationally—and their numbers continue to rise. Despite continued opposition in many quarters—Ohio is again a prime example—they've become a permanent part of the U.S. education landscape and a wonderfully versatile tool for reformers bent on creating educational options for needy kids, options that, all too often, the traditional system refuses or is unable to provide. And while Ohio remains something of a political outlier—a place where charters and other forms of school choice are viewed as GOP gimmicks—across most of America the charter strategy now enjoys bipartisan support, support that has strengthened since Barack Obama and Arne Duncan assumed their present posts in Washington.

2. Neither school choice nor results-based accountability is going away. More than 30 percent of U.S. children now attend schools other than their district-operated neighborhood school (it's up to 34 percent and rising in Ohio's Big 8 cities), and, if we include families that exercise choice via the real estate market—that is, that buy or rent in a particular neighborhood *because* of its schools—we are looking at a *majority* of young Americans. As choice mechanisms proliferate (now including virtual schooling, home schooling, and vouchers along with charters, magnets, and sundry intra- and interdistrict options), communities and parents are beginning to understand that educating children is not just something that bureaucratic systems do. It's something that parents select and shape for their daughters and sons—and can change and reshape when needed—much as they select clothes, food, churches, activities, and vacation destinations. But because society also has an interest in the education of its next generation, public policy—a blend of federal, state, and local—has begun to set standards, assessments, and accountability mechanisms by which to ensure that educational outcomes are satisfactory, whatever school or mode of schooling a family may elect.

3. The emergence of school choice and the onset of standards-based education have occurred with uncommon speed for major public-policy shifts and they've largely come from outside the public education system itself, often thrust upon it by elected officials, business leaders, aggrieved inner-city parents, and others concerned that the

traditional one-size-fits-all arrangement, containing few choices and little accountability, was not getting the job done, especially for poor and minority youngsters. A dozen years ago, Dayton had no charter schools, no private scholarships, and no publicly funded voucher program—and Ohio had no standards, statewide tests, or results-based accountability.

Now it has all of these, and the policy conversation is increasingly about how to make improvements to systems and schools within a framework that incorporates both choice and accountability. More than half of Dayton's children are availing themselves of school-choice opportunities. Today's big challenge there, and in cities like it, isn't to add yet more options but to ensure that those available to families are educationally sound. President Obama suggested as much when he told an Ohio reporter in early 2009, "the bottom line is to . . . make sure that we are maintaining very high standards for any charter school that's created."

4. Education is (and always has been) profoundly shaped by demographics and economics, but this doesn't mean we should give up on troubled urban areas. Ever since James Coleman's celebrated 1966 study showed that student achievement is strongly affected by nonschool factors, Americans have understood the manifold tribulations facing anyone bent on improving student achievement among our poorest children. There's no doubt that the saga of education reform in Ohio's cities is entangled with Rust Belt economics, poverty, job loss, fractured families, and the constant churning of children between schools. These pose grave challenges to schools and their children—and, perversely, these forces also tend to make educators more risk averse. In a community like Dayton, many of the remaining decent jobs are tied to the public schools. In such an environment, it is not surprising that people cling even tighter to what they've got and cast a wary eye on disruptive changes. This gets in the way of the very innovations and experiments that such communities urgently need if they're to rejuvenate themselves.

5. Yet risks need to be taken and changes embraced. Encouraging innovation, experimentation, and choice in K through 12 education entails obvious perils—and we fell victim to more than a few of them. Indeed, we ought to have looked closer at some of the charter schools we agreed to sponsor and otherwise tried to help. Sure, we should have been smarter about more of the elements that needed to be in place to optimize their chances of succeeding. We understand more clearly now just how many moving parts go into an effective school—and how vulnerable even the best of schools is to

disruption and deterioration when one or more of those parts break or vanish. But when half the children in many American cities don't graduate from high school, reasonable risks need to be taken. The status quo is totally unacceptable.

Essential Elements for a Successful System of High-Performing Charter Schools

6. Despite all the other influences in children's lives, really good schools make a big difference, particularly for poor and disadvantaged youngsters whose life prospects need a boost beyond what their families and neighborhoods can supply. In addition to academic skills and essential knowledge, they imbue children with goals and values, with confidence and determination. America doesn't have nearly enough such schools today. But it doesn't take many to demonstrate their value. The work of schools is surely easier when the rest of children's lives are in good repair, yet when other institutions are pitching in and other policy domains are aligned, schools alone can work wonders. And it's schools alone that are exclusively within the domain of education policy. We have no patience with those who insist that other changes must be made in society before schools can be expected to accomplish more for poor kids.

7. The schools and systems that work best for those youngsters are not all alike and are seldom static. They constantly seek improvement and they deploy funds, teachers, time, materials, and technology very differently. Ohio's handful of high-performing charters illustrates this diversity, as do high-performing schools across the land. Sure, there are commonalities across them. As analysts have observed since the dawn of "effective schools" research almost thirty years ago, they nearly always display strong cultures, astute and driven leaders, dedicated teachers, coherent curricula, shared responsibility, and a sense of common purpose. Yet each school also has its own personality and its own distinctive way of doing things. Successful schools know their students and address their needs. One of the strongest arguments for charter schools is that they are *expected* to be different.

8. The incentives need to be set right for everyone in the system: schools and their boards, operators and staff; sponsors and policymakers; and kids and families, too. Success needs to bring rewards; and failure needs to bring intervention, termination, and so on.

Everyone benefits from transparency and accountability, from having someone watching over their shoulder, giving them feedback on performance, and holding them to account for progress. Rewards can take many forms (promotions, accolades, bonuses, diplomas, etc.) and so can interventions (replace the principal, require summer school, put the school on probation, etc.). But nobody is better off when information is concealed, when self-interest trumps accountability, or when ill-considered financial incentives tempt one to tolerate—even expand—mediocrity. The charter arrangement in particular is a compact between a school and its sponsor. Properly structured, it rewards everyone for doing the right thing. Bungled, it invites mediocrity, avarice, underperformance, irresponsibility, and political attacks.

9. Incentives aren't enough without the resources to back them up. Strong bricks need sufficient straw. Charter enthusiasts (ourselves included) erred when they suggested that these new schools could surmount some of society's toughest educational obstacles on the cheap. Policymakers erred when they launched a fleet of new schools without the revenue, the facilities, or the expertise to reach their destinations. These new schools should receive the same support as the traditional kind. The principle here is simple: fund schools at the start according to the needs of the children attending them—and keep funding them (or not) on the basis of their performance.

10. It is practically impossible to have reliably good charter schools without competent, conscientious, properly motivated sponsors. Nationally, this is an underexamined and underattended realm, but in 2006 a national study found that "independent state charter boards and nonprofit organizations generally did a better job than others (including public school districts)." In short, the best sponsors are those that seek that responsibility and want to succeed at it. For the most part, that excludes school districts—with happy but extremely rare exceptions such as New York and Chicago. Yet this fact does not deter the established interests of public education from trying their utmost to restrict sponsorship to districts, nor did it keep Ohio lawmakers in 2009 from trying to provide more generous funding to district-sponsored schools than to independently sponsored charters. A move that ultimately failed, but only after a bruising political battle.

11. Good data really matter—and reveal important truths that are sometimes painful to behold. Education is so complex that even under optimal circumstances it's difficult to determine what is actually making a difference when it comes to academic achievement.

Besides basic factual data (how many students, how much money, how many teachers, attendance, graduation, etc.), the coin of the education-data realm is information on academic performance—which, of course, presupposes that someone has decided what performance is wanted and how to measure progress in relation to it. As detailed in this book, Ohio's schools have been undergoing nonstop school reforms since 1997 when the state created a framework of academic standards, tests, and school report cards. In 2002, the federal No Child Left Behind Act triggered more changes in every state's standards and accountability systems. Every such change takes time for schools and districts to assimilate and implement. Curricula have to be aligned to new standards, data systems have to be created to track and use the new student data, and teachers have to get up to speed on what these changes mean for classroom practices. Despite heroic efforts by groups like the national Data Quality Campaign, and despite millions of public and private dollars, few states and districts yet have the data they need, much less effective means of making the data accessible to teachers and parents.

12. Although innovation for its own sake has a dubious reputation in the education field—one recalls too many goofy fads and ill-considered brainstorms that didn't do much good and sometimes made things worse—innovating in pursuit of better education for needy children is an honorable and necessary quest. Despite hundreds of fine schools that serve poor kids in this country, despite evidence of commonalities across many of them, and despite the increasing capacity of some skilled operators to clone successful models in multiple locations, there is no magic formula. Because children and communities differ in innumerable ways, any given program or school design is apt to work better in some circumstances than in others. Family priorities differ, too, along with individual enthusiasms, learning styles, and—at least for now—state academic standards.

Replication is an iffy thing. We must, therefore, continue to welcome creativity and diversity in our education system. But we mustn't ever substitute innovation and diversity for results-based accountability. Getting that balance right is perhaps the greatest challenge that education reformers face.

What to Watch Out For, Guard Against, and Triumph Over

13. The education marketplace doesn't work as well as we believed—or as some of our favorite theories and theorists assert. It's supposed to result in parents selecting high-performing schools for their children while shunning low performers. In time, it should lead to either the improvement or closure of weak schools as the good ones gain market share. But in practice, really atrocious schools can languish for years when nobody intervenes. Too many families, particularly in troubled communities, simply aren't—or don't know how to be—very picky when it comes to choosing schools. They are wont to settle for such (admittedly important) basics as safety, convenience, and friendliness and not pay much attention to math scores, graduation rates, and college-going data.

    This problem is compounded by meager (or opaque) information about school effectiveness, a dearth of truly fine schools, a shortage of effective advisors and brokers, and the propensity of student-hungry schools to make claims that they may not live up to. Hence, another balance that needs to be gotten right in the new world of education choice is between a school's accountability to the parent marketplace and its accountability to school sponsors and other external monitors that focus single-mindedly on educational effectiveness.

14. Another important theory that softens in the fiery cauldron of reality is the assertion that, when a school fails to deliver the goods, sponsors and kindred authorities should just shut it down. This is an unshakeable part of charter school doctrine and we've proclaimed it a hundred times ourselves. Would that it were as easily done as said! But as anyone who ever tried to close or "reconstitute" a school has learned, sometimes to their great misery, even the worst of schools is usually the center of a loyal community of families, teachers, alumni and alumnae, friends, vendors, politicians, and others with a stake in keeping it open. Sometimes the school really *is* an institutional bulwark for a troubled neighborhood or an integral part of another vital—or well-connected—community organization.

    And sometimes—too often, in our experience—the school, mediocre as it is, is at least marginally superior to the other options within reach of its pupils. Under such circumstances, one doesn't lightly move to padlock that school. One first struggles to repair it. Except that's not easy, either, and there's a fine line between what a sponsor should do to help and what it must do to crack the whip. Our track record in this regard as a sponsor isn't great, and in fact we've had to place more hope in opening solid new schools than in fixing broken schools. Perhaps our biggest disappointment is that Ohio, like many other states, lacks expert "school doctors" and turnaround experts, and our own efforts to create such an enterprise—the k.i.d.s. organization in Dayton—fell victim to economics, personnel challenges, and other difficulties.

15. The sponsor-school relationship only works well when both entities hold similar values and priorities, up to and including their board members. That's true in good times and bad, but never more so than when a troubled school needs to be set right—or closed down. Fortunately for us, the schools we have worked to close had board members who agreed with us that the time had come. They shared our values and understood that doing right by children is more important than their own reputational or financial stake in schools they had struggled mightily to make work.

16. To our dismay, reformers and innovators can swiftly turn into their own vested interests with turf and jobs to protect. Some Ohio charter operators and sponsors have been blatant about this, which not only forfeits any moral high ground they might have claimed but also fractures the charter movement itself. Along with turf, money, and jobs comes concern about one's reputation, and reformers can be culpable there, too, particularly when they seek to rationalize weak school results. Too often we've heard, "These kids cannot . . ." or "Our scores may not be great, but our pupils come from broken families and you can't reasonably expect them to pass these state tests." Or, "Why should we be held to a higher standard than the crummy district schools?" For too many charter enthusiasts, *every* school is worth supporting *all* the time. Advocates stubbornly argue for "the right of all parents to choose" or simply stand on aggregate numbers that may conceal more than they illumine: "Ohio's charter schools provide a lifeline to more than 88,000 public school students and their families."

   The fact is, some charter schools are woeful choices for children and ought not to be defended. Yet they stay open year in and year out because neither their governing authorities nor their sponsors will do the right thing. This is why Republicans in the Ohio legislature, many of whom were longtime supporters of charter schools, passed an academic death penalty for terminally troubled charter schools in 2005. And this is why we and other supporters of quality charter schools urged them in 2007 and again in 2009 to toughen it. Of course it's unrealistic to expect those associated with any given school to welcome its death, yet leaders and strategists of the charter movement as a whole need to adopt the practice of triage: some schools are excellent as they are, some can be mended, and others are best left to perish.

17. Perhaps this is another example of naïveté, but we've never gotten used to—and hope we never truly accept—how often adult/institutional interests trump the interests of children. James Williams, the former Dayton superintendent who tried to convert his district's five worst schools into charters more than a decade ago, encountered the power of adult interest firsthand. His proposal was stymied by a teachers union that cared more about its members' job security. Most of the state-level political battles around education policy in which we've been embroiled have revolved around adult interests and money. The best interests of children rarely wield much influence.

18. Nothing lasting thrives in a hostile environment. Just as too many charter supporters are hung up on defending all charters all the time, their tireless opponents are bent on creating false distinctions and are constantly attacking them from every imaginable direction. Double standards and hypocrisy are in ample supply on both sides.

Final Thoughts

Eighteen lessons is a lot—but we've learned plenty over the past decade and there's no reason others should be condemned to repeat all our mistakes. Perhaps no other organization plays exactly the same mix of roles in its community and state as Fordham has found itself playing in Dayton and Ohio, and we don't suggest that any other setting is identical. But the country abounds in education reformers and charter school enthusiasts, and everyone can benefit from the experience of others, even when the circumstances aren't exactly the same.

One could come away from our war stories, our bruises, our should-haves and our wish-we-hads with a sense of futility. It's so hard to get all this right—is it really worth trying? Can it ever be done successfully?

But that would be the wrong conclusion. We're better at what we do in Ohio as a result of what we've learned through experience—and others will be better still. Other states have more salubrious political environments and other cities have superior leadership. Our own hats are off to (for example) what Michelle Rhee and Adrian Fenty are up to in Washington, what the KIPP team is doing in Houston, most of what Joel Klein has been struggling to do in New York, what Jeb Bush pulled off in Florida, what lawmakers in Colorado are striving to get right, what Paul Vallas and some heavyweight foundations are transforming in New Orleans, what the Mind Trust and school reformers are doing in Indianapolis to create better schools and attract more talent to education, and what a little band of charter backers have quietly brought about in Albany. Nor is that the full list. This is no time for despair. But it's also no time to reinvent wheels. The accumulation of school-reform experience in the United States is an invaluable knowledge base. Not all the lessons are happy, but all are instructive. Our purpose in these pages has been to add our bit to that growing body of understanding.

Celebrity policymakers aren't the only people we've come to admire in the course of our Ohio experience. We've learned to respect and value the hard work of teachers, school leaders, and board members who are working to make a difference in the lives of children who desperately need it. These individuals are real heroes, too often unsung and ill-compensated, and whether they work in a charter school, a district school, or a private school they deserve the solemn gratitude of all Americans. So, too, do millions of low-income parents who are doing their best against sometimes-staggering odds to give their daughters and sons the opportunity for a better future. We're honored to be their allies.

Notes

1. Stephen Koff, "Obama Backs Charter Schools for Cleveland," *Cleveland Plain Dealer*, March 1, 2009.
2. Louann Bierlein Palmer, "Alternative Charter School Authorizers: Playing a Vital Role in the Charter Movement," The Progressive Policy Institute, Washington, DC, December 2006, 2.

Appendix A

Glossary

Achieve, Inc. Bipartisan, nonprofit organization founded in 1996 by governors and CEOs to encourage and assist states in raising academic standards.

AFT. American Federation of Teachers, the second-largest teachers' union. Its major Ohio presence is in Cincinnati.

BES. Building Excellent Schools, a yearlong fellowship to train urban charter school leaders.

Bill and Melinda Gates Foundation. Large, private foundation established in 1999; education is a major focus.

Buckeye Association of School Administrators. Ohio's membership association of district superintendents and principals.

Center on Reinventing Public Education. Research and policy group engaging in K through 12 reform issues, founded in 1993 and presently housed at the University of Washington Bothell.

Charter School Authorizer (a.k.a. "sponsor" in Ohio). An entity that approves individual charter schools and is accountable for monitoring their performance vis-à-vis the terms of their charters as well as their compliance with applicable laws.

Coalition for Equity and Adequacy. Ohio-based coalition of school districts formed in 1990 to challenge the constitutionality of the state's school funding system.

Coalition for Public Education. Coalition of Ohio teachers' unions, the League of Women Voters, the Ohio PTA, the Ohio School Boards Association, and Ohio AFL-CIO.

Community schools. Ohio's official term for what other states call charter schools.

Council of Great City Schools. National organization based in Washington, DC, representing sixty-six large urban school systems.

DEA. Dayton Education Association.

DeRolph Case. Long-running lawsuit, first filed in 1991 by the Coalition for Equity and Adequacy, to challenge the constitutionality of Ohio's school funding system. Its proper designation is *DeRolph v. State.*

DPS. Dayton public schools.

Edison Project. Now EdisonLearning, Inc., a for-profit firm founded by Christopher Whittle in 1992 to develop a new model for U.S. schools.

Educational Excellence Network. Network of scholars, practitioners, policymakers, business leaders, and parents founded in 1981 by Chester E. Finn, Jr., and Diane Ravitch. The network's mission was taken over by the Thomas B. Fordham Foundation in 1996.

ERC. Education Resource Center formerly operating in Dayton, Ohio.

ESC. County Educational Service Center. Ohio has fifty-six ESCs, which vary widely in the programs and services they provide to local school districts and public charter schools.

IDEA. Federal Individuals with Disabilities Education Act.

k.i.d.s. Keys to Improving Dayton Schools, Inc.

Kids First. Quartet of reform-minded women, led by Gail Littlejohn, which won a majority of the seats on Dayton's Board of Education in 2001.

KIPP. Knowledge Is Power Program, a network of successful, college-preparatory charter schools, predominantly middle schools.

Lucas County ESC. Educational Service Center serving Lucas County, Ohio (Toledo), and one of Ohio's largest charter school sponsors.

NACSA. National Association of Charter School Authorizers.

National Alliance for Public Charter Schools. National organization committed to advancing the charter movement.

National Commission on Excellence in Education. Commission that authored *A Nation at Risk*, the influential 1983 report.

NCLB. *No Child Left Behind Act*, enacted in 2001, a reauthorization of the federal Elementary and Secondary Education Act with new provisions addressing academic standards, tests, and progress as well as teacher quality and other issues.

NEA. National Education Association, the country's largest teachers' union.

McKinsey & Co. Global management consulting firm producing reports such as *The Economic Cost of the U.S. Education Gap* and *Creating a World-Class Education System for Ohio.*

ODE. Ohio Department of Education.

OEA. Ohio Education Association. Ohio's largest teachers' union with about 130,000 members.

OFT. Ohio Federation of Teachers. Ohio's second largest teachers' union with about 20,000 members.

Ohio Alliance for Public Charter Schools. Nonprofit membership organization dedicated to the enhancement and sustainability of quality charter schools in Ohio.

Ohio Big 8. Eight largest Ohio urban districts: Akron, Canton, Cincinnati, Cleveland, Columbus, Dayton, Toledo, and Youngstown.

Ohio Charter School Sponsor Institute. Two-year project funded by the Thomas B. Fordham Institute, the Ohio Department of Education, the Bill and Melinda Gates Foundation, and the Walton Family Foundation, intended to recruit and support quality charter school sponsors.

Ohio Coalition for Quality Education. Advocacy organization for community (charter) schools.

Ohio Council of Community Schools. Nonprofit designee of the University of Toledo founded in 1999. It is one of Ohio's largest charter school sponsors.

Ohio School Boards Association. Member association of district school boards.

Ohio School Facilities Commission. State agency that administers Ohio's K through 12 public school construction program.

Ohio State Board of Education. Nineteen-member board (eleven elected, eight appointed by the governor), which creates policy and makes recommendations for K through 12 education in Ohio.

PACE. Parents Advancing Choice in Education. Dayton-based nonprofit organization providing scholarships for private-school attendance and other forms of assistance to families seeking to exercise school choice.

Phi Delta Kappa. International professional association for educators. It publishes *Phi Delta Kappan* and sponsors an annual survey of public attitudes on various education issues.

School Choice Ohio. Organization supporting Ohio's voucher program and providing information and outreach to eligible families.

Thomas B. Fordham Foundation. Philanthropic arm of the Thomas B. Fordham Institute and an Ohio charter school sponsor.

Virtual Charter School. Charter school that provides curriculum and instruction primarily via the Internet.

Walton Family Foundation. Private foundation established by Sam and Helen Walton with a major focus on school choice and other K through 12 education reforms.

White Hat. For-profit charter school operator, the largest in Ohio and third largest in the United States.

Zelman Decision. *Zelman v. Simmons-Harris* was a 2002 ruling by the U.S. Supreme Court (536 U.S. 639). It held that Cleveland's school voucher program (and others like it) did not violate the First Amendment's "establishment of religion" clause.

Appendix B

Key Moments in Ohio's Charter School Program

Date	Key Actions
June 1997 (signed into law) *Proposed in February 1997*	House Bill 215—established a pilot charter school program in Lucas County. The measure allowed for creation of both start-up and conversion charter schools, with the former permitted only in the Lucas County pilot study area. Conversion charter schools sponsored by traditional public school districts were allowed statewide.
August 1997 (signed into law) *Proposed in March 1997*	Senate Bill 55—expanded the charter school program beyond Lucas County, added the State Board of Education as a sponsor, and provided for the creation of start-up charters within the Ohio Big 8 urban districts.
1998	First charter schools open.
June 1999 (signed into law) *Proposed in May 1999*	House Bill 282—allowed for start-up charters in Ohio's twenty-one largest urban districts and, beginning in 2000, any school district deemed to be in Academic Emergency.
2002	State auditor Jim Petro released extensive report faulting ODE's oversight of the charter school program, urging that the agency get out of sponsorship, and recommending that other organizations—colleges and universities, county education service centers, nonprofit organizations—be approved as charter school sponsors.

Date	*Key Actions*
January 2003 (signed into law) *Proposed in September 2001*	House Bill 364—changed the State Board of Education's role from a sponsor of charter schools to the authorizer of school sponsors. The law permitted the state board to continue through June 2005 as sponsor of those schools it had previously approved, to allow them time to secure new sponsors. Sponsorship eligibility (for start-up schools) was extended to (1) public school districts; (2) county-level educational service centers; (3) the thirteen state universities offering four-year programs; and (4) qualified nonprofit organizations. All new sponsors were required to apply to the State Board of Education for approval. But any entity already serving as a sponsor on April 8, 2003, was grandfathered as an approved sponsor of start-up charter schools. House Bill 364 capped new start-up charter schools at 225.
June 2005 (signed into law) *Proposed in February 2005*	House Bill 66—expanded accountability for charter schools requiring that they report their special education and related services, as well as their expenditures for those services. The biennial budget bill placed two caps on the growth of charter schools (including limits on how many schools each sponsor could approve) and required that a lottery be held to determine the order in which new schools would be allowed to open. A moratorium was also placed on new e-schools. Despite caps, an operator that had already managed an academically successful charter school could open a new start-up school in Ohio.
March 2006 (signed into law) *Proposed in March 2006*	House Bill 530—determined that a charter school's governing authority members could not be employed by that school, nor have an interest in any contract awarded by the governing authority.

Date	Key Actions
October 2006 *Suit filed in 2001*	*State ex rel. Ohio Congress of Parents & Teachers v. State Bd. of Edn.* In a four-to-three ruling, Ohio Supreme Court upheld the constitutionality of state charter law, rebutting complainants' assertion that charter schools diverted funds away from public schools and were not part of the system of "common schools."
December 2006 (signed into law) *Proposed in February 2005*	House Bill 79—mandated closure of chronically underperforming charter schools. It also implemented a value-added accountability system for all public schools in Ohio and barred individuals from serving on the boards of more than two start-up charter schools at a time.
June 2007 (signed into law) *Proposed in March 2007*	House Bill 119—lifted the moratorium on new charter schools but stipulated they be managed by operators with a track record of success. (The governor's initial version of the state's biennial budget bill sought to kill the charter sector by imposing an ironclad moratorium on all schools regardless of operator quality; forcing all for-profit charter operators out of the state; imposing burdensome compliance, reporting, and teacher licensure rules on charters; and decreasing their funding by withholding parity and poverty aid.)
September 2008 *Suit filed in September 2007*	A state appeals court dismissed a lawsuit filed against a Dayton charter school by Ohio attorney general Marc Dann, who sought to shut down four low-performing charters in Dayton and Cincinnati (*State ex rel. Marc Dann, Attorney General v. Moraine Community School; v. New Choices Community School; v. Colin Powell Leadership Academy; v. Harmony Community School*).
July 2009 (signed into law) *Proposed in February 2009*	House Bill 1—placed all sponsors under the authority of the Ohio Department of Education, preserved funding for charter schools, and ratcheted up the automatic closure penalty for low-performing schools. (The governor's original version of the state's biennial budget bill would have cut charter school funding, added numerous regulatory burdens, and banned all for-profit operators.)

Appendix C

The Growth of Ohio's Charter Program, 1998–2009

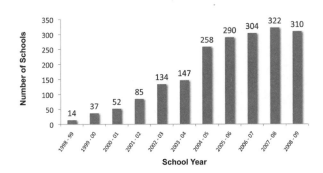

Figure C.1   Number of Ohio charter schools by school year

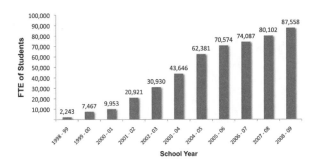

Figure C.2   Full-time equivalent (FTE) of Ohio students in charter schools by school year

Contributors

Chester E. Finn, Jr., is a scholar, educator, and public servant who has been at the forefront of the national education debate for forty years. Born and raised in Ohio, he received his doctorate from Harvard in education policy. He has served, inter alia, as a professor of education and public policy at Vanderbilt University, counsel to the U.S. ambassador to India, legislative director for Senator Daniel Patrick Moynihan, and assistant U.S. secretary of education for research and improvement. A senior fellow at Stanford's Hoover Institution and chairman of Hoover's Koret Task Force on K–12 Education, Finn is also president of the Thomas B. Fordham Institute and the Thomas B. Fordham Foundation. He serves on the boards of several other organizations concerned with primary and secondary schooling. He is the author of sixteen books, including *Reroute the Preschool Juggernaut* (Hoover), *Troublemaker: A Personal History of School Reform since Sputnik* (Princeton), *We Must Take Charge: Our Schools and Our Future* (Free Press), *What Do Our 17-Year-Olds Know?* (Harper & Row), and *Charter Schools in Action* (Princeton). Finn is the recipient of awards from the Educational Press Association of America, *Choice* magazine, the Education Writers Association, and the Freedoms Foundation at Valley Forge. He holds an honorary doctor of laws degree from Colgate University.

Terry Ryan is vice president for Ohio programs and policy at the Thomas B. Fordham Foundation (http://www.edexcellence.net). In this position, Ryan leads all Ohio operations for the foundation and its sister organization, the Thomas B. Fordham Institute, which include charter school sponsorship, grant making, and state research and policy efforts. He has lived and worked in Dayton since 2003 and has been close to the charter school efforts in that city and in Columbus. Ryan has served on the boards of the Ohio Charter School Association, School Choice Ohio, and the Keys to Improving Dayton Schools (k.i.d.s.) organization. He is a Stanford University's Hoover Institution Research Fellow and a 2008 New Schools Venture Fund/Aspen Institute Fellow. From late 1995 to November 2001, Ryan served as senior researcher for the United Kingdom–based 21st Century Learning Initiative. Ryan coauthored *The Unfinished Revolution*

(ASCD Press) with John Abbott. He received his master's degree from the University of Denver's Graduate School of International Studies in 1996, and as a Paterson International Fellow, he worked with school reformers in Warsaw, Poland in 1994 and 1995.

Michael B. Lafferty is a freelance science and education writer. A retired science reporter for the *Columbus Dispatch* newspaper in Columbus, Ohio, he was editor-in-chief of *Ohio's Natural Heritage*, a volume on the natural history of Ohio, and now serves as editor of the Thomas B. Fordham Institute's *Ohio Education Gadfly* newsletter. He is helping Fordham write a book on the institute's charter school experiences in Ohio.

Index